MW01599797

Just a small gift for you and your family on
behalf of Evangel Church.
We pray God's blessing on you as you
minister in God's Kingdom!

Seven Biblical Steps to Personal Renewal

LIVING IN THE SPIRIT OF REPENTANCE AND GRACE

A Devotional Study of the Seven Penitential Psalms

Volume 2 in the series
Songs From Life

Seven Biblical Steps to Personal Renewal

LIVING IN THE SPIRIT OF REPENTANCE AND GRACE

A Devotional Study of the Seven Penitential Psalms

Volume 2 in the series
Songs From Life

Rick C. Howard

Naioth Sound and Publishing
Woodside, California

Seven Biblical Steps to Personal Renewal
Published by:
Naioth Sound and Publishing
2995 Woodside Road, Suite 400
Woodside, California 94062
ISBN 0-9628091-6-0

Cover design and book production by:
DB & Associates Design Group, Inc.
dba Double Blessing Productions
P.O. Box 52756, Tulsa, OK 74152
www.doubleblessing.com

Editorial Consultant: Cynthia Hansen
                       P.O. Box 866
                       Broken Arrow, OK 74013

Printed in the United States of America.

Dedication

*T*his book is written to all who struggle with their Christian faith — to those who know the territory of repentance by heart.

I dedicate this book to those many men and women who have served with me on staff during more than thirty years of pastoral ministry. They have known my need for regular journeys into the heart of forgiveness. These vulnerable and selfless folk have been the persistent reminder of my weakness and the loving context for my change.

I also dedicate this book to my mentor and brother, Campbell McAlpine, and his lovely wife, Shelagh; to Deanna Duffy and Cynthia Hansen, fresh, new editors for my words; and, finally, to Christine and Richard Jensen, whose belief in me and this book project helped bring it from the heart to the printed page.

"I am a debtor."

*The needle of fear must go before the thread of love.
The needle punctures the place where the thread is to
enter, the needle is drawn out, the thread remains,
and holds the work together; so in penitence, fear
punctures the heart, and gives the Grace of Compunction, and love follows and by Contrition completes the
work, and binds the soul to GOD forever.*[1]

— Attributed to Saint Augustine

Contents

Foreword

*T*he contents of this book are life-changing, so handle with care. They are for contemplative consideration and not for speedy "surfing."

In *Seven Biblical Steps to Personal Renewal*, Rick Howard brings a necessary and urgent message for the present time. We are living in a period when there is a trivialization of truth, a triumphalism based on optimism instead of faith in facts, and a triteness toward the foundational basics of scriptural revelation.

It is therefore refreshing to hear the clear sound of the trumpet, with its echoes from the past, from the mouths of the prophets and apostles and from the Lord Jesus Himself. There is no uncertain sound in the message, nor multiplying of words; rather, a single word goes forth: *"Repent."* As John Milton rightly said, "Repentance is the golden key that opens the palace of eternity."

With scholarly skill, Rick expounds the truths he has gleaned from the seven Penitential Psalms of David. One feels the shock of David's exposé of his very soul — his confessions of sin, failures, weaknesses, fears, and helplessness; his self-inflicted wounds, as well as the wounds inflicted by both foes and friends.

For most of us, we sense an identification with David's feelings as we come to the realization that we are "creatures of like passions." Unfortunately, we may not always show the same willingness David did to acknowledge, confess, and repent.

This book reminds us not only of the sinfulness and foolishness of sin, but also of the glories and wonders of God's compassion, love, mercy, and grace. As you read, your heart will be stirred to praise and worship God for the redemptive work of the Lord Jesus, the preciousness of His blood that cleanses from all sin when we confess and repent.

One of my personal reactions in reading the manuscript was how appealing and attractive true repentance is. Rather than hearing an accusing voice or the thunder of condemnation, we hear only a Love that pleads and expresses a desire that we would know the greatest experience anyone can know on earth — intimate fellowship with God. When there is repentance toward God and faith in Jesus Christ, there is also the song of the soul set free and the restoration of the joy of our salvation.

A second impression given to me while I read this book was that of a person standing in darkness and despair. In the distance, a warm light beckons — a gracious invitation to repent and be revived as the steps of obedience are taken, with a beautiful sign that declares "Welcome Home."

Another result of reading the contents of this book is a deeper fear of the Lord — that reverential love for God that causes us to hate evil. Also encompassed in the fear of God is the dread of not accomplishing on earth what He has purposed for our lives.

David, the penitent one, the man "after God's own heart" (1 Samuel 13:14), earned the epitaph that he had "served his generation" (Acts 13:36). The application of the truths in this guide to personal renewal will enable us all to finish well.

Finally, I may have an advantage over many who read this book, for I know the author. He is a special friend. Behind what is written, I know something of his heart of compassion, his vulnerability, his honesty, his love for God, and his thirst to know Him. I know the church Rick has faithfully pastored for many years and the richness of his God-given ministry.

This isn't flattery or a man-pleasing statement; it is an honest assessment. Therefore, I know that I can listen to such a man, and I know that you can too.

Campbell McAlpine
Author of *Alone With God*
Worthing, England
January 2000

Why the Seven Steps?

*T*he title for this book comes from a quote in the *Word Biblical Commentary*: "In Christian tradition it [Psalm 143] has been regarded as the last of Penitential Psalms.... They represent seven rungs on the ladder of repentance...."[2]

This analogy does not imply a typical list of seven ideas. Instead, it guarantees a step higher in the truth of repentance and faith with the study of each Penitential Psalm. These seven Psalms are so designated both by their confessional nature and because of their use within the historic Christian community.

Preface

$\mathcal{D}$uring the last month of a one-year sabbatical, I was unexpectedly brought back to the San Francisco Bay area. Since I would soon be leaving again, I didn't want to prematurely reenter the environs of my home and ministry. So one Sunday morning, I visited Grace Cathedral in San Francisco. I have always loved that stately edifice. Although I had often walked through it, I had never attended a regular Sunday service there.

The relatively new (at that time) dean of Grace Cathedral, The Very Reverend Alan W. Jones, was speaking in that particular service. His message was not only pastoral but poignant as well. In somewhat of an aside, he defined the difference between a cathedral and a parish church.

"The Cathedral is a place for washing and eating," he said, pointing first to the baptismal font that greets the people when they enter the chancel and then to the huge central altar for Holy Eucharist or Communion that dominates the front of the building.

"The Cathedral," he continued, "stands *between* the secular world and God, offering Heaven's hospitality. You see, Heaven *is* hospitality!" his voice rang out. "The world is God's table, and diversity and conflict are inevitable."

Then he thundered (and Grace Cathedral makes such emphasis extremely obvious — almost theatrical): "This Cathedral is a place for *shared meanings* rather than *private desires*." What an awesome conclusion!

That is my hope for this book — "shared meanings." My prayer is that we might journey through the vulnerable and personal sharing of psalmists who keep redefining our own pilgrimage. These Penitential Psalms are a table of Heaven's hospitality. May our fellowship together in that hospitality be a spiritual refreshing that redefines the privilege of our walk with God.

Introduction

PART 1

'Repentance Seems Like Such Nonsense'

*D*o you often shudder at the use of certain words? Like tender flowers crushed beneath uncaring feet, some perfectly good words have been abused and dirtied along life's often dusty "word-road." For example, "gay" no longer means bright, happy or carefree. Today it is used to express a sexual lifestyle that is often grimly irresponsible.

"Repent" is also such a word. You can hardly speak it without conjuring up pictorial images of conniving, promiscuous Elmer Gantry-type sawdust preachers with hysterical, bulging eyes and a screaming, sensual display.

To others still, repentance is simply a spiritual "bummer" — an annual "downer-time" during which one must search for every error, dredge up every area of past activity, and endure a morbid, depressing recounting of sins.

Significantly, ever since the second century, a unique and very specific group of seven Psalms have been called the *Penitential Psalms,* or the *Psalms of Repentance.* There is even evidence that these particular Psalms were used together in Israel's experience as well. These seven Psalms will be the focus of this book.

Traditionally, the seven so-called Penitential Psalms are special material for Lent, the church's annual time of fasting and repentance (*see* Appendices 1 and 2). As such, these seven Psalms — Psalms 6, 32, 38, 51, 102, 130, and 143 — have almost universal acceptance.

You can easily find many slim volumes of study on the Penitential Psalms. Through the years, they have provided a platform for many famous teachers. My hope is to provide a simple manual for discussion and for each reader's personal pilgrimage into a deeper walk with God.

My personal goal in this series is easily discovered in the subtitle of this book, *Living in the Spirit of Repentance and Grace.* The true believer's life in Christ must always be a *lifestyle* and not simply a meaningless *ritual. Christianity must inevitably find its proof in experience.* The reflection of love that comes from stable and secure roots of spiritual acceptance is imperative for true joy.

The believer's earnest desire must be to produce an attractive, winsome life and a vibrant relationship with Jesus Christ for all the world to see. Apologetics, although seriously important, will never appear any more attractive than does the foundation of a house. Winsome, abundant *life* in God is the true decoration and the obvious attraction to those on the outside who observe the believer's spiritual "house."

Charles Haddon Spurgeon, who probably preached to more people, both in person and in print, than any man of his generation, frequently preached on mistaken notions about repentance. His concern was not only wrong ideas about repentance — such as morbid self-accusation, the dread of hell, or a sense of God's wrath — but also the unbelief, despondency, despair, and satanic attention these wrong ideas produced.

Like that great pastor-teacher, I am also concerned about mistaken views regarding the place repentance occupies in a believer's life. Repentance must never be seen as a means of procuring the grace of God, nor even as a preparation for grace itself. It should also never be viewed as a qualification or a gauge for a person's faith in Christ.

Repentance is never "spiritual wampum" to be exchanged at the eternal counter of God's merchandise mart! We cannot assume that God operates by the equation, "so much repentance = so much blessing."

"*Re*-vival" means "to restore to life." Jesus described the divine quality of that life in John 10 — it is life that is *abundant and free*. In the same vein, "repent" always speaks of a "turning." Actually, in the Old Testament, it more often refers to a "returning." Just the book of Hosea alone uses the word "turn" or "return" more than 18 times.

The call of God is always for us to *learn His ways*: "Who is wise, and he shall understand these things? prudent, and he shall know them? *for the ways of the Lord are right, and the just shall walk in them*: but the transgressors shall fall therein (Hosea 14:9 *KJV*).

How long does it take for us to fall from the wisdom of walking in God's ways? Our feasts run out of wine. The broken cisterns of our spiritual character let any *newness* leak out as quickly as it is poured in.

We are those who have known life; we have walked in the exhilarating "oxygen" of God's Holy Spirit. We have breathed cleanness and purity and have known the purposes of our God.

Then somehow the smog swells in — the suffocating, choking, yellow air of men's ideas, selfish ambition, and moral impurity. It always happens so gradually that we seem not to know the difference. Blue, open sky is quickly traded for yellow, brownish smog. The fresh, invigorating air of freedom soon becomes putrid and unhealthy.

For the believer reduced to this state of heart, repentance is to his life what exhaling is to the physical system. The human body must exhale the carbon dioxide in order to breathe in fresh invigoration.

That is also the "magnificent nonsense" of true repentance — not to procure or prepare for grace, nor to curry favor with God, but to prepare ourselves to receive fully the purposes, plans, and designs of God for our lives. Herein lies the true curriculum for repentance!

Jesus frequently called upon people to repent (turn around) because the Kingdom of God was near at hand (Mark 1:14,15). He warned them of the crusts of piety they had wrapped around themselves that kept them from changing.

Why did Jesus do this? Because He understood that repentance reverses our priorities and upsets our values. It "turns our pockets inside out," heralding a new life designed to cause us to release our old system of securities. Only then will we rush to grasp what at first seems to be a thin thread — *the purposes of God for our lives.*

PART 2

A Parable From the Cold War — The Relevance of Nonsense

I want to tell you a story out of a relatively simple spy-thriller called *Day of Judgment* by Jack Higgins. You may remember him for the book and subsequent movie, *The Eagle Has Landed*. Unfortunately, books are often better known than authors, with rare exceptions!

The year is 1963. There is an impending trip by President John Kennedy to Berlin — a visit the hard-line East German Communists want to *disturb*! A well-known Franciscan priest named Father Conlin, famous for running an escape route to the West, unwittingly falls into East German hands. Now they have their answer. Break Father Conlin; have a mock public trial; get him to give confirmation of CIA complicity; and so on. That will end the effectiveness of President Kennedy's trip.

The Vatican is helpless. Pope John XXIII is in his last dying moments, and neither the United States government nor West Germany can act officially. Then John Kennedy taps a 66-year-old Oxford professor of modern literature named Charles Pascoe for a daring "off-the-record" rescue attempt. It is a hostage drama with a predictable outcome.

You can already see that the book has everything! Professor Pascoe, incidentally, was a mastermind of MI-5, the British Intelligence of World War II. Amazing how a novelist can make everything fit!

There's a relatively unimportant sub-plot in the book. The Vatican decides to send a Franciscan priest, an ex-Notre Dame quarterback, into the village near where the Communists are holding Father Conlin hostage. The young Vatican priest and football player is Father Erich Hartmann. He is 33 years old, "extraordinarily handsome" (according to the author), a brilliant scholar, and incredibly strong. He comes under the guise of investigating the now-closed Catholic church in Neustadt, East Germany.

Hartmann's trip is really a way to inform the Communists that everyone knows they're holding Father Conlin near the village. Hartmann's role is relatively insignificant. It is actually a ruse to keep the Communist officials' attention off the real action — the plot to free Conlin.

Only someone forgot to tell Hartmann! When he gets to Neustadt, he finds a locked church and a village of spiritually hungry and needy people. The last priest at Holy Name Church in Neustadt had been Father Honecker — a much-loved and marvelous man, but 80 years old and very frail. His large and beloved congregation was an embarrassment to the Communist District Commander, so the District Commander devised a marvelous scheme. At this point, let me quote:

There was a famous cross at Holy Name, medieval, I think — named the Cross of St. Michael, in oak with a marvelous carving of our Savior on it. It stood in a stone socket by the altar. One night the District Commander had it removed and taken down to the bottom of the hill and planted in a grove of trees by the river. Father Honecker went to see the Communist officials and was told that the church stayed shut until the Cross of St. Michael was restored to its rightful place. The only stipulation was that Father Honecker had to carry it himself, which as the thing weighed around a couple of hundred pounds, was hardly likely.[3]

Of course, the old priest tried to carry the cross back to the church and thus died of a heart attack. It is in the aftermath of this scene that young Father Erich Hartmann arrives. He secretly takes confession, baptizes, and administers final rites. The rest is history — or in Jack Higgin's case, novel!

Father Erich Hartmann digs up the cross and, with almost superhuman strength, begins to carry it toward the church. Eventually the whole village turns out to watch. The weight of the cross and the steepness of the climb turn our young hero's body into one great ache.

The Communist officials come to the village, only to discover that a religious revival is on their hands. They can't let Hartmann succeed in returning the cross to the church, even though he is already starting up the church steps with his precious burden.

The ensuing skirmish ends with young Father Hartmann being shot, the cross unreturned, the revival quenched, and the church still shut. But, as I said, this is all a relatively unimportant sub-plot, although undoubtedly dramatic. The return of the cross is stopped by killing the upstart who would dare to restore it!

However, there is an interesting sidelight to this story. In Rome following the death of John XXIII, Montini is elected — who, by his own choice of name, will become Paul the VI. A conversation occurs in one of the Vatican's vaulted halls.

A priest asks, "Tell me, Father, what was Erich Hartmann really like?"

"Who knows?" replies the other priest. "A mystery, like all men, known only to his Maker."

"A bit of a Saint, would you say?" The first asks again.

"*Certainly not!* Erich was entirely lacking in the kind of humility needed for that office. *What he did at Neustadt was magnificent nonsense* — but thank God for it."

"Ah, well," the other priest answers. "I'll remember him in my prayers for the rest of my life."[4]

Magnificent nonsense, indeed!

Perhaps much of our lives as believers seems like magnificent nonsense to a casual observer. We want to return a cross to its central place in our life — not because we're saints but because we know it belongs there. That's increasingly the issue of our lives. It is as unalterably personal as the story I just related.

We all seem unprepared and not forewarned. But we seize the moment of a circumstance and begin a journey of choice. That's the challenge issued at the start of this study — not to simply learn in order to bolster our knowledge, but to *receive* in order to change our destiny.

God preserved this pilgrimage for us. We walk where multitudes of saints and sinners have gone before us. There will be a "cross" — a choice, a privileged moment. Who cares how it is observed by others in the long run? Our purpose is to pursue the intimate halls of relationship ourselves. We want, above all else, "to know Him."

Seven Biblical Steps to Personal Renewal

LIVING IN THE SPIRIT OF REPENTANCE AND GRACE

**A Devotional Study
of the Seven Penitential Psalms**

Volume 2 in the series
Songs From Life

PSALM 6

First of the Penitential Psalms

*Saint Hilary beautifully represents penitential
tears as going on an embassy to the Throne of Grace,
and this as the result. Another saint says, "The
prayers of tears are more efficacious than those of
words. Words of prayer often deceive, tears of prayer
never. A word is often unable to express its own
meaning, a tear can always say what it would."*[1]
— Quoted by A. G. Mortimer

CHAPTER 1

The Wail That Ends As a Song— The Chastisement of Love

Psalm 6

𝒫SALM 6

To the Chief Musician. With stringed instruments. On an eight-stringed harp.

O Lord, do not rebuke me in Your anger, nor chasten me in Your hot displeasure.

Have mercy on me, O Lord, for I am weak; O Lord, heal me, for my bones are troubled.

My soul also is greatly troubled; but You, O Lord — how long?

Return, O Lord, deliver me! Oh, save me for Your mercies' sake!

For in death there is no remembrance of You; in the grave who will give You thanks?

I am weary with my groaning; all night I make my bed swim; I drench my couch with my tears.

My eye wastes away because of grief; it grows old because of all my enemies.

Depart from me, all you workers of iniquity; for the Lord has heard the voice of my weeping.

The Lord has heard my supplication; the Lord will receive my prayer.

Let all my enemies be ashamed and greatly troubled; let them turn back and be ashamed suddenly.

*R*epentance is a lifestyle. It is a response of humility to a time when God convicts. That's all it is. That's exactly what it is. God's conviction is the faithfulness of the Holy Spirit to point out our wrong attitudes, words, or actions. Our part is to respond in humility rather than rationalizing and defending ourselves; to say yes to the Lord by immediately confessing the sin; to agree totally with the Holy Spirit as to the nature of that sin.

Repentance is to the believer's life what exhaling is to the physical system. Let's consider what this means.

On the average, each of us inhales 40,000 quarts of air a day. Given the current quality of much of our air, that fact alone is cause for some consternation! But the process of exhaling is as important as the process of breathing. We must exhale the carbon dioxide, the lifeless remainder. Appropriately, scholars of old used to call this carbon dioxide "fixed air," or stagnant air. We must rid ourselves of this stagnant air. We exhale that which has to do with death.

Repentance is the joy of the new and the elimination of everything lifeless. It is victory over stagnancy. To repent is to trade that yellow, brownish smog of men's ideas, selfish ambition, or moral impurity for the fresh, blue sky God provides — an open sky of cleanness and purity, where the divine purpose for our lives can soar high and free.

Not long ago, I read that the California Air Resources Board recently estimated up to 80,000 deaths per year occur through emphysema and other kinds of heart and lung diseases directly related to the smog present in California's air. Only God knows how many casualties occur because of the spiritual smog that clouds people's lives. His remedy? *Repentance.*

Only through repentance can the believer leave behind the shallow, unhealthy "breathing" that develops from unconfessed sin. Instead, he can exhale all that pertains to death and inhale God's life, enjoying the athletic, invigorating breathing that results from living in continual fellowship with God.

Getting Acquainted With the Territory of Psalm 6

The seven Psalms of penitence are really the stuff of new beginnings. They are the place of great comfort and victory, and none of the seven better illustrates this than Psalm 6, generally considered the first of the Penitential Psalms.

Dr. F. B. Meyer wrote this about Psalm 6: "The earliest verses are a wail, but the psalm ends in a song. It is like a day of rain which clears at evening."[2]

This is *not* the first impression of most readers of Psalm 6. Often the first time someone reads this Psalm, he quickly decides it will not be one of his favorites! Some phrases in this Psalm seem to virtually depress a person. Most writers, in fact, call attention to the fact that this is the lowest of the Psalms of penitence — the bottom rung on the penitential ladder, the lowest note on the penitential scale.

Psalm 6 *is* in some ways a low response of repentance. Its basis seems to be a simple desire to get out of trouble rather than a genuine basis of repentance such as true conviction or the character of God. The psalmist simply asks for his problems to end. Yet all of us can readily identify with this level of repentance as well.

First, I want to look at the introductory phrases of Psalm 6. They do in fact introduce the tenor of the Psalm itself.

The introductory phrase to this Psalm states, "To the Chief Musician. With stringed instruments. On an eight-stringed harp." The word translated as "stringed instruments" is the single Hebrew word *neginoth*. The phrase "eight-stringed harp" is the translation of a Hebrew word that simply means "eighth" and actually speaks of "an octave."

Some scholars say that most of these opening expressions are musical terms, since the Psalms were songs meant to be sung. Others believe that this is an instruction for the men in the choir to sing this Psalm one full octave lower than that of a normal voice range. This would certainly give the audience a feeling of the depth and dark nature of the words in this Psalm!

But let me share with you something else. Scripturally, eight is the number of "new beginning." The eighth day is the beginning or the first day of the week. Eight is also the sign of resurrection, which demonstrates the possibility of new beginnings. That's why we as Christians honor that day. Therefore, the "eight" used in the introductory phrase could signify the beginning of the divine process represented in this Psalm — a beginning that, although very low, leads to a victorious ending.

Most translations divide Psalm 6 into four stanzas. But if you examine the Psalm carefully, you'll discover there are only three stanzas, the second of which is longer by a third than either the first or the last stanza. I call your attention to this because it is important to note that the psalmist starts out with a cry of agony. The central portion then provides a working through of specific information. Finally, the psalmist and the reader come to a sense of great confidence at the very end.

The confidence at the end of this Psalm is one of the most important statements of confidence in God that's found anywhere in the Psalms. *This one fact should encourage you to dig deeper!*

Perhaps I should quickly admit a controversy about Psalm 6. Although for hundreds of years, Christians have called it a Psalm of penitence, the first of the seven Penitential Psalms, yet not once is there a mention of penitence in it! The closest idea to actual repentance in Psalm 6 is found in verse 4, where the psalmist asks God to return to him.

But perhaps we should review something on that very issue. In this case, we seem to be dealing with a psalmist who is not at all involved in deep sin. He is embroiled in difficult circumstances for which his own actions give him no explanation.

It is easier for all of us to handle adverse circumstances if we know we are the ones who got ourselves into the mess! We might tell ourselves, *All right, you did it. Now you're paying for it. That's the way it goes.*

On the other hand, one of the most difficult things in life is to be *misunderstood* or *misinterpreted*. We may act from a sincere and righteous heart and yet be totally misinterpreted by someone else.

Certainly that's true in our interaction with others. But the most difficult trial to endure in these moments is a seeming absence of God. We ask, "Why?" and receive only silence for an answer. There seems to be no explanation at all for the problems that have suddenly converged on our lives.

Many writers believe that David wrote Psalm 6 during his son Absalom's great rebellion against him. There certainly could be no darker moment in the history of David's life than that! David may very well have felt misunderstood by others and isolated from God at this time.

A crucial understanding of penitence is that it is not always related to some notorious area of sin. In a repentant moment, it is a believer's privilege to enter *by faith* into a greater realm of contrition and thus an understanding of God's dealings in his life.

Psalm 6 is in fact much like the book of Job. You may have thought of Job as you read the words. Job wasn't in trouble because he had sinned; he was in trouble because God thought highly enough of him to allow him to be tested.

Perhaps no literature in the Bible has been written about more than the book of Job. The story has been made into films, Broadway shows, and even science fiction books. Yet in reality, the key to Job is found in the New Testament: "Indeed we count them blessed who endure. You have heard of the perseverance of Job and seen the end intended by the Lord — that the Lord is very compassionate and merciful" (James 5:11).

Hallelujah! It is the *latter* end — God's ultimate intention — that counts! We must never lose that focus as believers. The Lord is compassionate and merciful indeed. We can praise Him for that. The latter end of life is in itself an important reason for studying Psalm 6.

Suppose you accept the thesis that this Psalm was probably written during a time in the psalmist's life when he had no legitimate conviction about notorious or unconfessed sin in his life. Suppose you also accept God's perspective of Job — that the latter end proved more important than the trials Job endured. When you accept these two premises, something else becomes important to you — the manner in which enemies (or perhaps I should say more softly, "people who simply don't understand") begin to add to a person's affliction through their use of proof texts and words of advice that don't fit the situation.

Does this sound familiar? It is so vital that we learn to keep our hands off other Christians and refrain from judging them! We have no idea what they're going through or why. Instead, let's pray for one another and allow God to finish His work.

'The Psalm of Sickness'

Psalm 6 has been called by some a *Psalm of sickness*. Within its three stanzas are references to physical affliction, physical terror, insomnia, tears, trembling bones, and a weak body. Of course, we must understand that, as with all the Psalms, this Psalm was written under the Old Covenant. The psalmist's understanding reflects the limited knowledge of God that people possessed before the New Testament.

For example, the writer to the Hebrew Christians declares in essence, "You have come by such a better, easier way than God's people under the Old Covenant did! You haven't come trembling to the mountain of fire and tempest as they did. You have come through the blood of the Lamb and the revelation of the New Covenant" (Hebrews 12:18-24). Indeed, the very privilege we possess to confidently approach the throne of the Father and receive forgiveness is a better way!

For example, anyone reading Psalm 6 is struck by the fact that this psalmist obviously doesn't possess a New Testament hope of resurrection. "...In the grave who will give you thanks?" he asks (verse 4). In other words, he is saying, "Lord, You better heal me now, because the only way I'll be able to praise You is to finish living my life on this earth. There is no praise to You in the grave."

The word for "grave" here is *Sheol*, used about 85 times in the Old Testament. Almost half those times, this Hebrew word is translated "death." All the other times *Sheol* is used, it is translated "hell." Needless to say, that in itself can be very confusing.

The New Testament clearly declares that through Jesus Christ, the issues of life and immortality came to light: "But has now been revealed by the appearing of our Savior Jesus Christ, who has abolished death and brought life and immortality to light through the gospel" (2 Timothy 1:10).

What a privilege to live on this side of the Cross and the revelation in Jesus Christ! Yet we read about the lives of such great Old Testament heroes as Abraham, Moses, Esther, Samuel, and Hannah. How great indeed their faith had to be in order to walk with so little revelation about immortality!

There is to be more rapture in death for us as Christians than in any other experience. Jesus said in John 14:3 that He would come personally and take us unto Himself. What glory for each of us to anticipate! But why do we possess this revelation of glorious hope? Because it is received through Jesus.

The man in Psalm 6 is under difficult circumstances, and enemies are taking advantage of his circumstances. He can't relate the experience to anything he has done specifically, yet he knows he is sick.

Have you ever tried to be spiritual when you're sick?

Moments of real sickness make devotions difficult. For instance, I am told that as Augustine lay dying, he asked for Psalm 32 to be painted on the wall facing him so he could see its words and meditate on its truth. Psalm 6 speaks to all of us about just those kinds of life experiences.

The Trials and Sorrows Through Which the Godly Pass

Let's look at the first stanza of Psalm 6:

O Lord, do not rebuke me in Your anger, nor chasten me in Your hot displeasure.

Have mercy on me, O Lord, for I am weak; O Lord, heal me, for my bones are troubled.

My soul also is greatly troubled; but You, O Lord — how long?

Psalm 6:1-3

In this first stanza, the psalmist recognizes that there are actually two kinds of judgments. One is a judgment of mercy that we might call *chastisement*. This is for the purpose of edifying and strengthening the believer. Then, of course, there is also the *just wrath of God*. I know it isn't popular in this day and age to speak of that, but God's wrath toward evil is as important as His love. It is the flip side of the coin, the balance of God's character.

However, this psalmist's plea seems to be as follows: "Lord, I understand chastisement, and I respond willingly to it. I also understand that if You wanted to blot me out, You could. I am not worthy to be in Your presence. Nevertheless, I pray for mercy, not justice."

The word "bones" in verse 2 and the word "soul" in verse 3 are actually related to the same word. Both words probably describe physical problems as well as spiritual causes.

As we know today, psychosomatic diseases are diseases of the body that are caused by the mind. Today we even talk about *somopsychic* diseases. This is an entirely new field of medicine, dealing with the many aspects of mental anguish that may be caused by imbalances and problems within the physical body. We are discovering that the body can affect the mind as profoundly as the mind can affect the body.

This psalmist seems to say, "God, You have a right to blot me out. You are righteous, and wrath is part of Your character. I acknowledge that, but I pray for mercy. I'm willing for You to bring chastisement into my life. I'm willing for You to change me. It is *not* difficult for me to respond to Your discipline as a Father."

Hebrews 12 says a lot about chastisement. In fact, it says that if you don't have any, you're not a son or a daughter (verse 8). You're illegitimate. You're not really in the family.

The only people who are sons and daughters are those who show evidence of God's discipline at work in their lives. Therefore, the entire first section of Psalm 6 is very important.

A Request and a Prayer

The second stanza is longer by a third than the first: "Return, O Lord, deliver me! Oh, save me for Your mercies' sake! For in death there is no remembrance of You; in the grave who will give You thanks?" (verses 4,5).

The psalmist follows this plea by saying, "I am weary with groaning. My bed is literally swimming. (That's exactly what it says in the original Hebrew!)

I drench my couch with tears. My eyes are wasting away with grief. They are growing old because of my enemies" (verses 6,7, author's paraphrase).

These are interesting verses about *inner* life experiences. They present a picture of humiliation and repentance, of enduring suffering yet questioning it as well.

During the latter days of John Calvin's life, he adopted the words from verse 3 as his own: "O Lord — how long?" Calvin frequently spoke these words when he could no longer pray or keep the disciplines he was used to practicing. Over and over again until his death, Calvin repeated these words, "O Lord — how long?"

Calvin must have felt physically worn out, just as this particular psalmist obviously did. The psalmist speaks of weeping, insomnia, and physical weakness. In fact, he reveals a kind of hopelessness about death. Included in that frustration is the thought that when he dies, his opportunities with God will be over!

The wasting and the loss the psalmist has suffered are particularly personified by his *eyes*. His eyes have been so given to weeping that they have begun to degenerate: "My eye wastes away because of grief; it grows old because of all my enemies" (verse 7).

Still, the psalmist's ultimate concern is about God: "For in death there is no remembrance of You; in the grave who will give You thanks?" (verse 5). Again, this is spoken from the psalmist's limited Old Testament understanding. The sentiments of this verse are changed totally through Jesus Christ. Now Paul writes, "We are confident, yes, well pleased rather to be absent from the body and to be present with the Lord" (2 Corinthians 5:8). Instant presence! No sleep of the dead!

In fact, when a believer goes to be with the Lord, he or she is more alive than ever! Never talk about departed believers in the past tense. To die and be with the Lord is instant. We miss them, of course, and we mourn the loss of their actual fellowship in which we can touch and relate to them. But they are more alive in that moment than they have ever been. In fact, it is the celebration of the end for which all of life is lived!

However, don't pass by an important key in this Psalm. In verse 4, the psalmist gives us the basis of his prayer. The *New King James Version* reads, "...Oh, save me for Your mercies' sake!" The Hebrew word for "mercies" here is *hesed*, which means "covenant love" or "longsuffering kindness" — the central quality of God's character.

Now this brother is getting down to business. He knows *how* to pray! He is saying to God, "I'm not going to stand before You and defend myself on the basis of the good works I've done. I'm not going to recite a litany before You of everything good I've done in my past and then ask You to do something for me! I know better than that. I deserve nothing from You. But for the sake of Your own character, Lord, and on the basis of the covenant You've made with me, I come to you.

"You are a God of longsuffering and mercy, and I pray for Your salvation to come to me because of Who *You* are, not because of what I am! I pray for You to save me from sickness and from death."

God Will Respond

Then between verses 7 and 8, the psalmist hears something in his spirit. There's a rustle, a wind moving in the trees.

Nothing has actually changed; he's still sick and weeping. But it's obvious he has heard something when he says, "You workers of iniquity, those of you who are standing by taking joy in this, you'd better turn tail and start running now, because the Lord has heard the voice of my weeping! He has heard my supplication, and He will receive my prayers. Then my enemies will be ashamed and troubled, and they will be turned back and ashamed suddenly!" (verses 8,9, author's paraphrase).

Now here's an interesting thing! Did you notice that the psalmist repeats, "the Lord *has* heard" twice and then says, "He *will* receive my prayer"? Do those verb tenses trouble you? Some translators try to correct this by making *all* the phrases in the perfect tenses. Grammarians call this "the perfect of certitude."

Although his bodily disease is not yet lifted, nor the dark, hostile words of his enemies removed, this psalmist has heard God's whisper of assurance, and it has changed his spirit! He knows the hour for his deliverance has now been determined. It is already for him a certainty!

This is a scriptural demonstration of faith. You see, faith is never the manipulation of God in order to receive an answer to prayer. We don't approach a spiritual counter of merchandise and present a measure of faith or repentance so we can receive something in exchange. It isn't a matter of "exercise this much faith — receive this miracle or healing." That's clearly manipulation, not faith!

Faith is knowing that God has made everything that is seen out of that which is invisible, simply through His Word (Hebrews 11:3). Through the ages, many people have simply said, "Hogwash!" to this scriptural statement. However, man's discovery of the atomic and molecular structure of the natural world has made that Bible truth easier to understand. Modern physicists now add their own words of confirmation, saying, "It's true — whether you're talking about animate or inanimate life, all matter is based on this invisible molecular structure."

Therefore, based on God's lovingkindness, faith declares, "I have cried these words to Him; He has heard me; and it is just a matter of time until the response comes!"

Many of us wait until we experience a phenomenal release in our spirit — an inner sense of our prayers being answered — before we will say, "I now have this in my hand." We often say, "I'll know I have it when I can touch it, taste it, feel it, or sense it. That's how I'll know."

That's pragmatism, the overriding principle of the twentieth and the twenty-first centuries. But true faith is a violent opposite of pragmatism. Pragmatism and faith do not mix well; they're like oil and water.

Faith is the certitude of God's righteous character. I hang my life on faith and say, "That's it! I don't have to see it; I don't have to taste it; and I don't have to touch it. It's *fact*, and it's settled!" We miss so much when we don't push through to the moment of knowing this truth — receiving it, living in it, being changed by it!

Imperative Applications

Are we ready for the truth? If so, we must recognize that there is a school of adversity in which we all must ultimately become students. We may not learn very well while experiencing only God's goodness, grace, and unconditional love. However, we all learn wonderfully in the school of discipline and adversity.

One phrase in Psalm 6:8 absolutely stops the reader in his tracks: "the voice of my weeping." This phrase reminds me of Paul's words in Romans 8:23: "Not only that, but we also who have the firstfruits of the Spirit, even *we ourselves groan within ourselves*, eagerly waiting for the adoption, the redemption of our body."

All of us are aware of our incompleteness. We wish to be complete, so we groan with utterances that only the Holy Spirit can make through us. Thus, we each become a voice of weeping in a school of adversity as we respond in brokenness and humility. Indeed, everything in such a place must depend on the mercy and faithfulness of God.

There is a marvelous New Testament story about a loving minister who had poured more of his life into a certain congregation than any other group of people he had ever ministered to. Yet this church produced some of the most carnal responses recorded in the Bible the first time the minister's back was turned. In fact, one response was so sinful, even nonbelievers would not have allowed it in their midst!

The specifics involved a young man in the congregation who was living in the worst kind of an immoral relationship, incestuous by its very nature. This minister's heart was torn. First, he received a personal visit from someone who informed him of the problem, prompting him to return to the congregation. Later, a letter was sent to him, telling him even more sordid details.

The minister responded with a strong letter of correction to the church leadership. "Look," he wrote, "you either get this situation in order, or the next time I visit you, it will have to be with a rod and not with love."

The congregation was stirred up, convicted of heart. The adversity produced fruit, and the Word produced results. The people responded to the Holy Spirit's conviction in humility and repentance. In fact, their repentance was so marked that the same minister had to quickly write another letter and say, "Enough already!"

In the midst of this correspondence is a description of repentance we would do well to memorize. The apostle Paul, the minister in this story, wrote to the Corinthian church:

> Now I rejoice, not that you were made sorry, but that your sorrow led to repentance. For you were made sorry in a godly manner, that you might suffer loss from us in nothing.
>
> For godly sorrow produces repentance leading to salvation, not to be regretted; but the sorrow of the world produces death.
>
> **2 Corinthians 7:9,10**

How can we test the difference between godly sorrow and the sorrow of the world? The next verse helps clarify this point.

> For observe this very thing, that you sorrowed in a godly manner: What diligence it produced in you, what clearing of yourselves, what indignation, what fear, what vehement desire, what zeal, what vindication! In all things you proved yourselves to be clear in this matter.
>
> **2 Corinthians 7:11**

There is a type of sorrow that may appear religious but is in fact the sorrow of the world. It includes grief over being caught and the search for a way of escape. It is a pragmatic use of repentance as a way to get out of the results of judgment. Worldly sorrow produces death. Godly sorrow, however, brings true repentance and change. That's how we can test the difference.

I suppose if the psalmist of Psalm 6 were to say anything directly to us, he'd tell us, "There is no circumstance — whether or not understood, whether or not people are using it against you — that cannot be surrendered to God on the basis of His covenant, His faithfulness, and His love. Only on that basis of surrender will difficult circumstances produce brokenness and blessing!"

Perhaps weeping is a lost discipline among many Christians. I certainly see little of it in the Church. Now, I'm fully aware that weeping can be morbid or overly introspective. Perhaps there was a time when we felt as though we had to weep at every Communion service, just as we ended every service with an altar call. But shall there now be a time when we are always dry-eyed? Is that not actually a worse state for the Church to be in?

Do you ever remember when there was such a cleansing of your heart, such a restoring of zeal, diligence, and brokenness that you walked into the next day of your spiritual life as if you were walking into a world that had just been refreshed by a beautiful rain shower? What a difference! Such a world seems so fragrant, aromatic, clean, and pure.

Everyone should know the difference between fragrance and freshness and the stagnancy, dryness, and lethargy of an unbroken life. But some folks *don't* know that difference. They just endure a smog-filled continuation of activity without a joyous participation in life.

Perhaps the worst thing that can happen to someone is to not know the difference. A person can struggle in many ways in life, but it is only when he loses this sense of perspective that his struggle becomes fatal and his weaknesses propel him toward death.

Who is repentance for? It is for us as believers. Who is revival for? It is for us as believers! We are to come to God with the consistent desire for wholeness and newness of life in Christ Jesus.

Respond in Repentance

Perhaps as you read this, you are being quickened to a genuine sense of repentance in some area of your life. If you sense a true, humble response to the Holy Spirit's conviction in your heart, an important process has begun in your life.

You may be far ahead of other Christians in your spiritual sensitivity. Nevertheless, God has put His finger on certain areas of sin and transgression and said, "That can't continue. That can't go on in your life if you want to continue growing in your relationship with Me."

Allow me to close this chapter with some very specific advice on this particular phase of repentance. First, don't ever allow anyone else to judge where you are. Don't allow it to be someone else's responsibility to say to you, "I've received this or that for you." Allow only the Holy Spirit to be the Governor of what is happening in your life right now.

Second, whatever you find yourself walking through at work, within your family, or in any other area of your life, know this: Nothing touches your life but that has come to you either through God's purpose or through His allowance.

Therefore, use the situations you face for your betterment. *Frame this moment in your life* by saying, "Lord, I don't even need to understand all this. Here's my mess — my broken dreams, my lack of understanding, my concerns, hurt and confusion. I lift all of it to You, Lord, and I say that, within the framework of these circumstances, I want to begin to receive a greater understanding of Who You are and what You wish to do in my life.'"

Third, for the Lord's sake and for yourself, push beyond the mundane mediocrity of an average response. Don't be afraid to wail before the Lord; don't be afraid to be honest before Him and to cry out. If you want to, shake your fist at Him and say, "Lord, I don't understand. Why is this happening?"

Always be honest with God. Remember — it's all part of "exhaling." If you hold in your pain and your feelings of resentment, bitterness can become lodged in your spirit. So let your hurt and struggling emotions find expression before the Lord. You'll discover He always has a way of responding back to you.

Last, make sure your response to the Lord is based on His lovingkindness. Don't begin your response of repentance so the Lord can show His faithfulness to you. Begin your response *on the basis of* His faithfulness.

Say to Him: "Father, because of Your covenant love, because of Jesus Christ, because of all He is, because of what He is to You — on the basis of all this, I come into repentance. This year by Your grace, I'm going to let this wheel begin to turn — this conviction of my heart — and I promise to respond in humility."

You might continue with a prayer something like this:

Father, I thank You for this opportunity for a new beginning through Your Spirit of grace and godliness. I come to You to repent, to break open an area of my life as an alabaster box. I pray that You would be blessed by the fine aroma of my heart's conviction as I respond in repentance to You.

Lord, I open my life to You right now. You see my circumstances, both physical and emotional. I lift up to You the inexplicable circumstances of my life, even those that have caused others to turn away from me. I give You all these arenas.

My cry to You is based on Your lovingkindness. I ask that these circumstances would produce brokenness and repentance in my life. I want to breathe out and rid myself of everything that is unhealthy, stagnant, bitter, and contrary to the character of Jesus Christ. Also, Lord, by Your grace I begin to breathe the invigorating and renewing air of the Holy Spirit, to bring new life and new purpose into my life.

———————

And thus this first great Psalm of penitence, the lowest of the seven steps in the ladder of repentance, fitly ends with hope of pardon for the penitent, and with a prayer for the conversion of the impenitent, an act of faith in our own forgiveness, and a prayer for the companions of our sins. It is the lowest in the scale of Penitential Psalms, since its key is the minor one of Fear; but 'the Fear of the Lord is the beginning of Wisdom,' Psalm cxi.10, and who so wise as he who repents![3]

PSALM 32

Second of the Penitential Psalms

In conventional phrases, it may be, but with a deep spiritual fervour that redeems and beautifies the whole, the songs that thrill the psalmist's heart are now to be caught up and chanted by the entire Church. For in this grand "Hallelujah Chorus" of exultant adoration and praise, the penitence of the pious in Israel is to be glorified.[1]

— John Adams,
The Lenten Psalms

CHAPTER 2

Learning From Your Life

Psalm 32

$\mathscr{P}$SALM $\mathscr{32}$

A Psalm of David. A Contemplation.

Blessed is he whose transgression is forgiven, whose sin is covered.

Blessed is the man to whom the Lord does not impute iniquity, and in whose spirit there is no deceit.

When I kept silent, my bones grew old through my groaning all the day long.

For day and night Your hand was heavy upon me; my vitality was turned into the drought of summer. Selah

I acknowledged my sin to You, and my iniquity I have not hidden. I said, "I will confess my transgressions to the Lord," and You forgave the iniquity of my sin. Selah

For this cause everyone who is godly shall pray to You in a time when You may be found; surely in a flood of great waters they shall not come near him.

You are my hiding place; you shall preserve me from trouble; you shall surround me with songs of deliverance. Selah

I will instruct you and teach you in the way you should go; I will guide you with My eye.

Do not be like the horse or like the mule, which have no understanding, which must be harnessed with bit and bridle, else they will not come near you.

Many sorrows shall be to the wicked; but he who trusts in the Lord, mercy shall surround him.

Be glad in the Lord and rejoice, you righteous; and shout for joy, all you upright in heart!

One type of Psalm listed in several divisions of the Psalms is called a Wisdom Psalm, or a didactic Psalm. Psalm 32 is one of these. It is considered to be one of the Psalms of ascent and of special focus to us in this study. It is also the second Psalm of the seven Penitential Psalms.

In my view, Psalm 32 is the clearest and most teaching-oriented of all Psalms in the Psalter. This particular Psalm gives clarity and definition to the concept of repentance. It is by its very circumstance a costly demonstration and a vulnerable personal illustration of how repentance is walked out in the individual believer's life. I plead with the reader to spend special personal time in this chapter, since it so perfectly outlines and patterns repentance for every believer's experience.

King David's 'Finding Time'

I must begin by saying, as one must often do, "Thanks to David and the faithful Holy Spirit in his life!" We are privileged to learn so much from David through spiritual "osmosis" and by application to our own lives.

If what I am about to relate were a fairy story, I might begin with something like "Once upon a time." However, the circumstances of this true account don't permit me to be so glib.

Long ago, a spiritually sensitive king named David decided to retreat from a normal time of warfare and luxuriate in his own security. One morning during his self-imposed "retreat," he looked across the battlements of his castle and lusted for the beautiful Bathsheba. He ultimately took her to his bedchamber in the absence of her husband, Uriah, and became sexually involved with her. A few weeks later, an emergency note was sent to the castle from the house of Uriah. The note was from Bathsheba, secretly informing David that she had become pregnant.

David must have paced the floor as he tried to think of a solution. Finally, he decided to bring Uriah off the battlefield. Incidentally, although Uriah was a Hittite, he was one of the first to join David in his early struggles for the kingship. In fact, Uriah was one of David's most loyal commanders and personal friends.

Perhaps this is an excellent time to review a very basic idea. David was not suddenly overcome by uncontrollable lust when he happened to look over the battlements and see Bathsheba taking a bath. We sometimes get that idea when we hear this story told. Uriah had been a close associate of David, similar to the close working relationship between business associates or fellow pastors on a pastoral staff. The wives of David's close associates were familiar and known.

Nowhere does the Bible teach that sin is a sudden slip or an irreversible fall. We constantly hear people say, "I fell in love," or "I fell out of love," as though falling in love is as sudden and accidental as slipping on an icy street on a winter afternoon. People love or lust by deliberate choice. They choose whom to love, and they choose whom not to love.

The Bible says in Romans 13:14, "But put on the Lord Jesus Christ, and *make no provision* for the flesh, to fulfill its lusts." No one sins without planning it! So never think this was an instantaneous, momentary happening in David's life. The seeds of the sin had been sown in associations over a period of years.

Finally, David made plans to bring Uriah off the battlefield. David asked Uriah how Joab, the commander over his army, how he was doing, how the people were doing, and how the war proceeded. Then he suggested that Uriah go to his home. Uriah went home all right but stayed all night at the doorway. When David asked why, Uriah replied, "...The ark and Israel and Judah are dwelling in tents, and my lord Joab and the servants of my lord are encamped in the open fields. Shall I then go to my house to eat and drink, and to lie with my wife? As you live, and as your soul lives, I will not do this thing." (2 Samuel 11:11).

David's carefully thought-out plan had been thwarted by the very loyalty of this man! He scribbled a hasty letter to Joab, put the seal of the king upon it, and gave it to Uriah. What he wrote is almost unprecedented in its cruelty: "...Set Uriah in the forefront of the hottest battle, and retreat from him, that he may be struck down and die" (2 Samuel 11:15). This was deliberate, premeditated murder, and it happened exactly in that way. David then took the widow, Bathsheba, into his own household. The rest of the story you probably know.

This experience became a "finding time." The Lord sent the prophet Nathan to David. Nathan was more than just a prophet; he was a friend of David. Both he and Gad had been David's school roommates. Together they had studied under Samuel, each for his own ordained role in the history of Israel.

Nathan told David a story about a man who had one little lamb that was more family than animal to him. Across the road lived a man with an enormous ranch and thousands of cattle and sheep upon his hills. When a friend visited the wealthy man, the man insisted on taking his poverty-stricken neighbor's one special lamb to slay for dinner rather than taking one from his own huge flock of sheep.

David's anger was greatly aroused against the man in the story, and he said to Nathan, "As the Lord lives, the man who has done this shall surely die!" (2 Samuel 12:5). Isn't it amazing how excited we can become over someone else's sin? Here was an adulterer who had just murdered a best friend but was now ready to kill a man who took a neighbor's lamb!

All legalism is such a dead-end trip. First, it always imposes the legalist's standards on someone else's life. Secondly, it provides the legalist with a false sense of security. Having maintained a certain set of standards, he sees himself as somehow righteous. This tragic Old Testament story is the product of that kind of an experience.

Nathan replied, "...You are the man! Thus says the Lord God of Israel: 'I anointed you king over Israel, and I delivered you from the hand of Saul. I gave you your master's house and your master's wives into your keeping, and gave you the house of Israel and Judah. And if that had been too little, I also would have given you much more!'" (2 Samuel 12:7,8). What an incredible verse! How similar to all of us under grace!

Nathan continued:

> 'Why have you despised the commandment of the Lord, to do evil in His sight? You have killed Uriah the Hittite with the sword; you have taken his wife to be your wife, and have killed him with the sword of the people of Ammon.
>
> 'Now therefore, the sword shall never depart from your house, because you have despised Me, and have taken the wife of Uriah the Hittite to be your wife.'
>
> "Thus says the Lord: 'Behold, I will raise up adversity against you from your own house; and I will take your wives before your eyes and give them to your neighbor, and he shall lie with your wives in the sight of this sun.

'For you did it secretly, but I will do this thing before all Israel, before the sun.'"

So David said to Nathan, "I have sinned against the Lord." And Nathan said to David, "The Lord also has put away your sin; you shall not die.

"However, because by this deed you have given great occasion to the enemies of the Lord to blaspheme, the child also who is born to you shall surely die."

Then Nathan departed to his house. And the Lord struck the child that Uriah's wife bore to David, and it became ill.

2 Samuel 12:9-15

What happened after Nathan departed? David pleaded with God for the child born to Bathsheba. He fasted; he went in and lay all night upon the earth, refusing to get up or to eat. But on the seventh day, the child died. The servants of David feared to tell him the child was dead, for they said, "…Indeed, while the child was alive, we spoke to him, and he would not heed our voice. How can we tell him that the child is dead? He may do some harm!" (2 Samuel 12:18).

Instead, when David knew the child was dead, he arose from the ground, washed and anointed himself, and changed his clothes. Then he went into the house of the Lord and worshiped. Later, he requested food in his own house, and he ate. His logic, as told to the servants, was very revealing: "…While the child was alive, I fasted and wept; for I said, 'Who can tell whether the Lord will be gracious to me, that the child may live?' But now he is dead; why should I fast? Can I bring him back again? I shall go to him, but he shall not return to me." (2 Samuel 12:22,23).

Still later, David comforted Bathsheba. What a sign of real manhood! David didn't indulge in the "macho" blaming of Bathsheba's feminine lures for what had happened. Here was a man who, in the finding time of God, had developed such maturity that in the midst of this crisis, he went to his wife and comforted her.

And look carefully at the result of David's maturity: Out of that moment of acceptance and compassion, a son was born. The child was named Solomon, which means "peaceable." That can't be just a coincidence. David's correct response produced an answer both for his future and for that of his nation.

Real peace is always the fruit of following the finding time of God to its ultimate end. Notice the next issue in the story. Joab defeats the people of Ammon. Then David returns to his proper place of leadership among the people and helps them take the royal city of Rabbah, meaning "the city of waters" (2 Samuel 12:29).

Rabbah was the second most important city to Jerusalem itself. It was David's second greatest victory militarily, and it came on the heels of this finding time. David had responded correctly to the Holy Spirit in the process of that experience.

This story can rightly be called background material for Psalm 32. It is truthfully the introduction and explanation of God's gracious provision and His use of a time of true repentance to bring about positive change.

This is a great place to stop and do some personal inventory. David does not stand alone as he bears consequences from circumstances of his own making. However, his response marks an unusually high order for each of us to follow.

Establishing a Standard for Repentance

With this background for Psalm 32 in mind, we have yet one more necessary preliminary to our study — the 51st Psalm. Although we study this Psalm later as one of the Penitential Psalms, it is important to note that

Psalm 51 was David's first response following Nathan's visit to him.

We know well so many of the phrases of this famous Psalm:

Have mercy upon me, O God, according to Your lovingkindness; according to the multitude of Your tender mercies, blot out my transgressions.

Wash me thoroughly from my iniquity, and cleanse me from my sin.

For I acknowledge my transgressions, and my sin is always before me.

Against You, You only, have I sinned, and done this evil in Your sight — that You may be found just when You speak, and blameless when You judge.

Behold, I was brought forth in iniquity, and in sin my mother conceived me.

Behold, You desire truth in the inward parts, and in the hidden part You will make me to know wisdom. [Underline that in your heart: "You will make me to know wisdom!"]

Purge me with hyssop, and I shall be clean; wash me, and I shall be whiter than snow.

Make me to hear joy and gladness, that the bones You have broken may rejoice.

Hide Your face from my sins, and blot out all my iniquities.

Create in me a clean heart, O God, and renew a steadfast spirit within me.

Do not cast me away from Your presence, and do not take Your Holy Spirit from me.

Restore to me the joy of Your salvation, and uphold me by Your generous Spirit.

Then I will teach transgressors Your ways, and sinners shall be converted to You.

Psalm 51:1-13

In a very real sense, both Psalm 32 and 51 are Christian psalms. In other words, although the world is blessed by them, they apply particularly to the believer's experience.

Psalm 51 is the ejaculative prayer of David. He falls on his face before God and confesses his sin to the Lord. There are so many heart cries here: "Don't cast me away. Don't take Your Spirit from me. Teach me wisdom. You desire truth in the inward parts. Lord, make the bones You are now breaking rejoice before you."

Yet it is as though David suddenly gets an inspiration. He prays, "O God, if You bring me through this finding time, I'm going to become *an instructor* in righteousness. My experience is going to be the 'broken bread and poured-out wine' before others! Then they also may understand in a finding out time how to respond before You, O God!"

God has always made provision for sin — through the laws of sacrificial covering and ultimately by putting away sin once and for all through Jesus Christ. The eternal issue has always been belief in and obedience to God's provision: "He who believes is not condemned," to paraphrase John 3:18.

The unbeliever insists on paying for sin himself throughout eternity with his unbelief. On the other hand, the believer has accepted the payment for sin, which is ultimately Calvary! Nevertheless, the believer who accepts this journey of maturity and change must learn the consequences of sin in his life and ministry.

It is the believer we are talking about in Psalm 51 and Psalm 32. God only "searches and tries the ways" of the believer. In regard to unbelievers, the Holy Spirit will only convict of sin, righteousness, and judgment and bring them to a knowledge of Jesus Christ. But after a person comes to Christ and accepts the payment for sin, he knows once and for all the nature of God's payment for sin!

Hebrews 9:26 says that "...now, once at the end of the ages, He [*referring to Jesus Christ*] has appeared to put away sin by the sacrifice of Himself." Colossians 2:13,14 says, "And you, being dead in your trespasses and the uncircumcision of your flesh, He has made alive together with Him, having forgiven you all trespasses, having wiped out the handwriting of requirements that was against us, which was contrary to us. And He has taken it out of the way, having nailed it to the cross."

The issue is no longer sin, as though God must do something *else* to bring forgiveness to us. Nevertheless, it is God's desire in the stewardship of our lives to correct the floundering of our experience through failure and sin.

God isn't shocked by any sin that any believer is now practicing or has ever committed. God dealt with sin *realistically* in the life of Jesus Christ and *sacrificially* through the offering and death of Jesus Christ.

God isn't shocked. But He *is* concerned that we continue to learn and grow toward maturity. God isn't willing to allow any of us to stagnate in immaturity. He has a dream and purpose for us that is above anything we can comprehend. And He is continually finding us out so that we do not rest in a lesser position than He intends for us.

Meanwhile — Back to Psalm 32!

In the first two verses of Psalm 32, David calls sin by three different names, all of which are important. The first is *transgression*; the second is *sin*; and the third is *iniquity*. Transgression most often describes "that which breaks a relationship." This obviously refers to a believer's experience, since a nonbeliever cannot transgress a relationship that has never existed! Transgression speaks of the heart-wrenching reality of an important relationship that has been broken.

Perhaps the greatest empirical evidence that proves we truly are believers is our reaction when something in our lives interferes with our fellowship with God. The moment our fellowship with God becomes clouded, an immediate cry should arise in our spirits: "O God, don't cast me away; don't take your Spirit from me!" As true believers, we understand that our relationship with God is so vital and precious.

But secondly, David calls his failure *sin*. In the original Hebrew, this means "that which is crooked or perverse." We know there is a straight law of God's righteousness — the law of His holiness. When we cast down beside that straight law of God something that is serpentine and crooked, we immediately recognize the difference.

Every day in our lives, some word, motive, attitude or activity can be found crooked when placed in reference to the purity and straightness of Who and what God is. Just like David, we need to acknowledge it as sin.

But David also saw his activity as *iniquity*. "Iniquity" is the primary word for sin in the Old and New Testaments. Both in the Hebrew and the Greek, this primary word means "to miss the mark; to fall short of the purpose of God." I believe this is the ultimate concern of our God.

Never view God as someone who sits up in Heaven, sadistically creating laws we can't keep, delighted when we break them so He can arrive on the scene with His rod of judgment. Never! He is a God who has called us into eternal fellowship. He wishes to reveal the ultimate purposes of Jesus Christ to us; He has a dream for what we can be. He is heart-broken when He sees us falling short of His ultimate intention for our lives.

I must say it again — legalism is a dead-end trip. We may take delight in the fact we don't drink, swear, spit, chew — or even go with those who do! But is any of that the central issue in God's sight or in our lives? Perhaps God's concern is a root of bitterness, a word spoken against a brother, or our failure to step into the specific calling God has given us. His primary concern could even be that we feel inferior when He has instructed us to be courageous! In other words, God's main concern is whatever causes us to fall short of *His purpose* for our lives.

David begins this 32nd Psalm with the word "blessed." Literally, he says, "Oh, the blessednesses (plural) of the forgiven." Jesus often used the word translated "blessed" or "happy" as well.

What's the end result of a finding out time for a believer who learns to respond correctly? "Happy is that man!"

By the way, Psalm 32 also ends with the word "rejoice," a word often translated "to dance." Don't make this difficult to comprehend. God wants to restore a true and joyful dance to your life in the completion of His dealings with you.

What Happens When We Confess

"Transgression," David says, "is forgiven." The original Hebrew literally says that transgression is *lifted off* us. That which hurts a believer the most is the sense of brokenness in his relationship with God. God says, "I will lift that sense of brokenness off you and restore our relationship."

The sin, or the crookedness, in our lives is covered and atoned for. That is also good news! In addition, our iniquity will never be imputed or counted against us.

This is such a marvelous promise that the apostle Paul expounds on it in his great chapter of faith, the fourth chapter of Romans. Making justification by faith imaginable in man's experience, Paul calls out the good news, "Blessed is the man to whom the Lord shall not impute sin" (Romans 4:8)!

God doesn't impute against us our missing of the mark. However, Paul challenges us to know that not only does God *not* impute our unrighteousness, He also imputes *to* us righteousness by faith: "But for us also, to whom it *[righteousness]* shall be imputed, if we believe on him that raised up Jesus our Lord from the dead" (Romans 4:24 *KJV*).

Has your bank account ever become overdrawn? Imagine if a wealthy friend in your city went with you to your bank and told the bank official, "Whenever a debit comes into that person's account, take the debit off *my* account. Also, I want you to transfer $1,000 once a month from my account to his!"

"I sure wish that would happen to me!" you might say. Dear friend, consider this: God doesn't impute your unrighteousness and iniquity to you, but He *does* impute His righteousness to you. Such a deal!

Perhaps now you understand what David is saying in Psalm 32. He is saying, "Look, the ultimate issue wasn't my sin. Obviously, I fell short of God's purposes. I confess it as a crooked transaction against the holy Law. It broke the relationship I've always enjoyed with a holy God. We couldn't be in the open relationship we had enjoyed prior to that moment.

"But when God brought about a finding out time, He helped me respond correctly. He lifted from me the brokenness of our relationship and covered the crookedness of my way. He imputed the iniquity, the missing of the mark, to His own account." What a revelation this is!

44

Response Is Really the Issue

David teaches us in Psalm 32 that at least three responses are possible in a time of failure. (Remember, this Penitential Psalm is *not* spontaneous but a careful, deliberate teaching.)

David's first response to the vital issues God was dealing with him about was *silence*. But David warns us that negative things happened when he kept silent. First, he explains, "...my bones grew old through my groaning all the day long. For day and night Your hand was heavy upon me..." (verses 3,4).

David's first reaction of silence and hiding from his sin brought about a physical result. We, too, often harbor resentments that need to be confessed or avoid dealing with past actions for which there needs to be restitution. These are issues that must be corrected before God. When we keep silent, the Word of God says we grow old.

The original Hebrew here suggests that the bone structure of David's life began to resemble that of an old man. His body began to sag; his shoulders became stooped. Premature age started to come upon him.

Isn't it possible that many churches will never change or grow until the local body of believers takes responsibility for that church's past? Entire churches need to come before God and search out their history, repenting of the way they have treated ministers or of activities that have been carried out in the flesh rather than by the Spirit of God.

Even our attitude toward other members of the Body of Christ in our community is relevant to our spiritual health. We must always guard against feelings of superiority or of judgment toward other believers.

I believe we begin the process toward a premature death when our response to a finding out time of God is not adequate nor correct. Isn't this the meaning of Paul's comment in First Corinthians 11:30 when he writes, "For this reason many are weak and sick among you, and many sleep"?

This warning is directed toward believers. I believe sincerely that God's Word teaches He ends some believers' lives prematurely because of their wrong response to the discipline of the Holy Spirit. David certainly was aware of this. He seems to be saying, "Premature death was working in my life!"

Next, note the phrase, "Your hand was heavy upon me" (Psalm 32:4). Judges 2:15 records, "Wherever they went out, the hand of the Lord was against them for calamity.... And they were greatly distressed."

The hand of God is not against unbelievers in this life. It is only heavy against believers who refuse to walk openly before the Lord when they are convicted of sin. Why, my friend? Just back up to the divine motive. *Because He loves His children, and His is a tough love!* When the Holy Spirit convicts, repentance is the only appropriate response.

Hebrews 12 deals thoroughly with this subject of God's chastisement in the believer's life. It is often taught as though it refers to Daddy taking a switch to the place of Junior's rebellion. However, it is interesting to note that chastisement in Hebrews 12 is the Greek word *paideio*, which usually doesn't mean the rod at all. It refers to all a loving father does to plan the maturity of his son — the entire moral context of a father helping his son grow up according to what he considers best. This includes situations in which the dad refuses to rush in to solve a problem for his child because he knows it's time for the child to learn how to solve the problem for himself.

46

Many times a good dad must stand with his arms folded, leaving his child to endure the experience even when it hurts him. Oh, friend, *that is the real chastisement* we are talking about. David found the chastisement, or the hand, of God heavy upon him. God's love for him would not let him stay immature.

David further writes, "...my vitality was turned into the drought of summer" (Psalm 32:4). In place of the word "vitality," the literal language says, "The sap of my life." Perhaps we would say, "The vital issues of who and what I am suddenly stopped functioning!"

I remember well the day a fine young Christian musician came to my office. He had written a lot of Christian music and was widely received in the Body of Christ.

"Rick, I don't understand it," he complained. "I'm not receiving any new music from the Lord anymore. I used to write two or three good songs every week. Some of those are now sung all around the country. But the flow has stopped!"

I replied, "There is one primary reason why creative energy dries up in a Christian. What's going on in your life that God is dealing with you about and you're not responding correctly to? Is there an issue of moral impurity?"

Often we ask the question, "What known sin is in your life?" In a way, that question is inadequate. To most of us, sin is a deliberate activity we willfully became involved in. But, of course, the Bible's definition of sin is broader: "All unrighteousness is sin..." (1 John 5:17). Then in Romans 14:23, it says, "...whatever is not from faith is sin." Finally, Romans 3:23 says that to sin means to "...fall short of the glory of God."

"The hand of God was heavy upon me," David wrote, "and the vital sap of my life dried up." Can you imagine David trying to play on his harp, only to have every note seem discordant? The words of life that used to flow by the inspiration of the Spirit now seemed dead and stagnant. It was as though God was saying, "David, I will not permit you to continue finding spiritual comfort in your nice little worship expression when you are refusing to acknowledge your situation."

In a word, God turned off the valve, and the creative juice stopped. *To David, it was like a spiritual drought.*

I pray intently that you can apply this truth to yourself and to others right now. It is so easy to perform religious activity in the energy of the flesh. We continue to do work for God, but the authentic flow of inspiration has ceased! And why has it ceased? Because God has placed us in a finding out time, and our response has not been pure before Him.

In sharp contrast to the first few verses of Psalm 32 is verse 5, where David cries out victoriously, "I acknowledged my sin to you, and my iniquity I have not hidden. I said, 'I will confess my transgressions'..." (Psalm 32:5).

I'm sure you can see that the order of verse 5 is exactly the reverse of the order of verse 1. In verse 5, it is first *sin*, then *iniquity*, and finally *transgression*.

David continues, "For this cause everyone who is godly shall pray to You in a time when You may be found *[literally, "a finding time"]*; surely in a flood of great waters they shall not come near him" (Psalm 32:6). Repentance comes during a time of "finding out." A change must take place in your life because God loves you and requires you to walk out the process.

You remember from Second Samuel 12 that David prayed for his baby to be spared. The intensity of his emotion as he fasted and prayed brought fear to the hired servants. However, when the baby died, the issue was settled. David got up, washed and anointed himself, went into the house of God, and worshiped. Later David asked to eat, having finished that important stage of repentance.

David speaks about God in such wonderful ways in the continuation of Psalm 32. God is preserving him, encompassing him about with songs of deliverance! This is the victory of honest response to God's conviction.

In verses 8 and 9, a dramatic switch takes place in the Psalm. God is so pleased with David's response that the Holy Spirit breaks into the Psalm Himself. The subject changes, and the Spirit of God directly and prophetically says, "I will instruct you and teach you in the way you should go; I will guide you with My eye" (verse 8). What a promise to a penitent!

Oh, there's nothing that brings as much joy to the Father as the believer who, during a time of divine discipline, responds brokenly and in true repentance!

The Father will turn on the searchlight in each of our lives, putting us in a "finding time" when He deems it necessary. And when our response before Him is right, He is so pleased that He breaks in and promises: "From now on, I am going to guide you, teach you, and lead you." *Oh, how wonderfully worthwhile true repentance is!*

But not all believers respond so well! David warns, "Do not be like the horse or like the mule, which have no understanding, which must be harnessed with bit and bridle, else they will not come near you" (Psalm 32:9). The phrase "bit and bridle" is actually "bit and muzzle" in the original Hebrew. The meaning speaks for itself!

Perhaps nothing is more important in church life than understanding this fact: No one is more dangerous than a bitter Christian who is unresponsive to the dealings of God. Pray that such people do not come near you.

Now I want you to ponder carefully what I'm about to tell you. What are believers like who don't respond correctly to God in a finding out time? Again Hebrews 12 gives an answer. They are those who, during that finding time, let their hands hang down and their knees get thrown out of joint (Hebrews 12:12,13).

The writer to the Hebrews then goes on to say, "Looking diligently lest anyone fall short of the grace of God; lest any root of bitterness springing up cause trouble, and by this many become defiled" (Hebrews 12:15). This speaks of a very real negative possibility. A Christian who doesn't respond the way God desires while he's in a finding out time may find that his experience makes him bitter and troublesome. Watch out for that Christian!

The entire implication of David's sin or any believer's sin is that the world surrounding them is negatively affected. I am absolutely convinced that many believers literally poison their families and churches with this wrong kind of response during a finding out time. Just one root of bitterness magnified in a congregation of several hundred produces tragic results — all because of someone's lack of a correct response. That person wasn't willing to say, "God, You have allowed this situation. I've confessed my sin, and now I move on." Instead, bitterness springs up in him because God's hand is against him and creative energies have slowed to a halt.

Another Christian to watch out for is the fiercely loyal church worker who is actually driven. He will do any job, but you better carefully clear the way ahead of him! These Christians will sometimes substitute activity for repentance and brokenness. They need to be muzzled — they're dangerous when they get too close! But the greater tragedy is in their own unchanged, unrenewed minds and lives.

Psalm 32 ends by saying, "Many sorrows shall be to the wicked; but he who trusts in the Lord, mercy shall surround him. Be glad in the Lord and rejoice, you righteous; and shout for joy, all you upright in heart!" (verses 10,11).

What an ending! God promises unimaginable release and blessing to His children who correctly respond. This, my friend, is God's guarantee to the believer whose heart is open to Him.

Never deny the Lord an opportunity to prove His faithfulness to you. You are called to walk in an infinitely fresh and inviting new life. Repentance is the open door to that new life. It is the call to a glorious new release, an amazing new beginning!

A Prayer of Repentance

My Father, You are the One who puts me in these finding out times. You want me ready for the ultimate finding time in eternity. But I often struggle with You in these moments of my life. May the sweet and gentle work of Your Spirit suddenly make the Word true, basic and understandable to me.

Lord, I have no other reason to live. Of what importance is living in a house or owning possessions? You are the great Steward of my eternity. You've chosen me for a purpose. You know my gifts, functions and ministry. I am indeed a dream You have conceived in Your heart, and You are heart-broken when I fall short of that purpose.

In the finding out time I face right now, in this *kairos* moment of my life, I want to lift it all to You. Thank You, Father, for godly sorrow that works in me repentance. Thank You, Father, for dealing with me, for not letting me get away with my carnality and immaturity.

Oh, Father, how You love me! You love me so much that You plan the whole discipline of my spirit. You raise me as Your child.

Order my life by Your Word. Don't let sin have dominion over me. Thank You, gracious Father, for the clarity and work of your Spirit. I yield to that work now with thanksgiving — not in condemnation, which is what the enemy brings, but in genuine conviction through the loving surgery of Your Holy Spirit. I know You will restore me, setting bones in place.

Lord, circumstances may be dark around me, but there is no darkness in You. I surrender. In the finding time of Your Spirit, I say an eternal yes to you, O God. I will fast, pray, and repent. I will not let anyone prostitute this moment in my life. When it is ended, Father, I will get up, wash myself, anoint my face and hands, and go on in Your eternal purposes. By Your grace, I will become broken bread and poured-out wine from Your own vineyard. Thank You for this in Jesus' Name. Amen.

PSALM 38

Third of the Penitential Psalms

The eye can see more than the lips can ever utter. The tears of the contrite are sweet in the eyes of God; the weeping of a penitent heart is acceptable to the Almighty as the only offering He can receive. So in that bitter bath of hot and blinding tears, Peter was transformed and reborn. In after years Peter had occasion to bless God for the burning experience of that dark hour. Peter came out of the Crucible of Calvary, saved.[1]

— Harry Rimmer,
The Crucible of Calvary

CHAPTER 3

The Arrows of God
and the Road to Healing

Psalm 38

$\mathcal{P}$SALM $\mathit{38}$

O Lord, do not rebuke me in Your wrath, nor chasten me in Your hot displeasure!

For Your arrows pierce me deeply, and Your hand presses me down.

There is no soundness in my flesh because of Your anger, nor any health in my bones because of my sin.

For my iniquities have gone over my head; like a heavy burden they are too heavy for me.

My wounds are foul and festering because of my foolishness.

I am troubled, I am bowed down greatly; I go mourning all the day long.

For my loins are full of inflammation, and there is no soundness in my flesh.

I am feeble and severely broken; I groan because of the turmoil of my heart.

Lord, all my desire is before You; and my sighing is not hidden from You.

My heart pants, my strength fails me; as for the light of my eyes, it also has gone from me.

My loved ones and my friends stand aloof from my plague, and my relatives stand afar off.

Those also who seek my life lay snares for me; those who seek my hurt speak of destruction, and plan deception all the day long.

But I, like a deaf man, do not hear; and I am like a mute who does not open his mouth.

Thus I am like a man who does not hear, and in whose mouth is no response.

For in You, O Lord, I hope; you will hear, O Lord my God.

For I said, "Hear me, lest they rejoice over me, lest, when my foot slips, they exalt themselves against me."

For I am ready to fall, and my sorrow is continually before me.

For I will declare my iniquity; I will be in anguish over my sin.

But my enemies are vigorous, and they are strong; and those who hate me wrongfully have multiplied.

Those also who render evil for good, they are my adversaries, because I follow what is good.

Do not forsake me, O Lord; O my God, be not far from me!

Make haste to help me, O Lord, my salvation!

It has been said, "With peace in his soul, a man can face the most terrifying experience; but without peace in his soul, he can't manage even the simple task of writing a letter." That's a very good understanding with which to begin looking at Psalm 38, the third Penitential Psalm.

The seven Penitential Psalms have been identified as a way of moving into the sufferings of Christ and of denying oneself. Psalm 38 has been identified as one of these seven Psalms since the second century of the Christian church. Specifically, this Psalm identifies a time of trouble, yet also provides an assured reason for hope.

How do we look at trouble? The answer to that question may tell us more about ourselves than anything else in our lives.

Norman Vincent Peale used to talk about an old Irish tradition that said whenever there was trouble on the earth, it meant there was movement in Heaven. Then Peale would tell about an old Irish preacher who used to say, "When I see problems on earth, I rejoice because I know there is movement in Heaven, and that will ultimately mean greater things for earth." That's certainly a healthy way to look at the troubles that can arise in life!

On the other hand, problems cause some of us to act as though God were dead. A little girl named Harriet once wrote to God, "Dear God, are You real? Some people don't believe it. So if You are, You'd better do something quick!"

Isn't that like most all of us? We ask, "How can God allow this?" or "Why doesn't God do something quick?"

Let's establish this fact *before* our study of Psalm 38: God *cares*. He cares a lot. And what's more, He isn't frustrated. Joy Dawson, a famous Christian speaker, frequently says, "God is as relaxed as a poached egg!" Although God is the most *intense* Person in the universe, He is not one bit *tense*.

In his letter to the Thessalonians, the apostle Paul wrote, "In everything give thanks; for this is the will of God in Christ Jesus for you" (1 Thessalonians 5:18). Simply put, everything means *everything*! When things go well or when life seems difficult; when we understand the circumstances we face or when we question them — no matter what, in *everything* we are to give thanks.

It isn't that Christians are blind to difficulties or insensitive to issues of injustice. They know as intensely as anyone else the nature of pain in human existence. Nevertheless, both spiritually and mentally, Christians are supposed to affirm the *goodness* of God in every situation.

We trust in God's providence. It is our privilege to see the cup as being half full, not half empty. We emphasize that *all* things are possible through Christ and that the Christian life is meant to be filled with blessing. *There is every reason in the world to be hopeful.* Why should we dwell on the difficult? Instead, in everything we can give thanks, because by God's grace and power we are more than conquerors through Christ Jesus!

The Psalm Itself

Let's prepare for this important study by actually reading Psalm 38. *Please do not skip this part.* This is where we establish the context for important things the Holy Spirit will teach us!

At issue in this Psalm is a major sin that has become too heavy to bear (verses 3,8). The psalmist feels God's wrath and seems to collapse in physical pain. At the same time, his spirit languishes in deep depression. His enemies use the occasion to plot against him, and even his friends stand apart and aloof from him.

The psalmist seems too sick to respond. In his pain, he can only cry out to God. Here indeed is a man hanging on to God by a shoestring — by a thread! But as he bares his soul, we learn the steps toward healing.

This Psalm includes some of the Bible's most profound expressions — words that speak to a place hidden deep within all our spirits.

O Lord, do not rebuke me in Your wrath, nor chasten me in Your hot displeasure!

For Your arrows pierce me deeply, and Your hand presses me down.

There is no soundness in my flesh because of Your anger, nor any health in my bones because of my sin.

For my iniquities have gone over my head; like a heavy burden they are too heavy for me.

My wounds are foul and festering because of my foolishness.

I am troubled, I am bowed down greatly; I go mourning all the day long.

For my loins are full of inflammation, and there is no soundness in my flesh.

I am feeble and severely broken; I groan because of the turmoil of my heart.

Lord, all my desire is before You; and my sighing is not hidden from You.

My heart pants, my strength fails me; as for the light of my eyes, it also has gone from me.

My loved ones and my friends stand aloof from my plague, and my relatives stand afar off.

Those also who seek my life lay snares for me; those who seek my hurt speak of destruction, and plan deception all the day long.

But I, like a deaf man, do not hear; and I am like a mute who does not open his mouth.

Thus I am like a man who does not hear, and in whose mouth is no response.

For in You, O Lord, I hope; you will hear, O Lord my God.

For I said, "Hear me, lest they rejoice over me, lest, when my foot slips, they exalt themselves against me."

For I am ready to fall, and my sorrow is continually before me.

For I will declare my iniquity; I will be in anguish over my sin.

But my enemies are vigorous, and they are strong; and those who hate me wrongfully have multiplied.

Those also who render evil for good, they are my adversaries, because I follow what is good.

Do not forsake me, O Lord; O my God, be not far from me!

Make haste to help me, O Lord, my salvation!

Psalm 38:1-22

One Sunday night years ago, I sat spellbound in front of my television set, watching and listening to the painful, tearful confession of a leading American evangelist. He said, "I do not plan in any way to whitewash my sin or to call it a mistake. I call it a sin, and I beg your forgiveness."

The minister's 20-minute, emotion-packed appearance before that weeping congregation was far from specific. But he did make it clear that the sin he was dealing with was not a one-time occasion, but a lifetime of practice since his youth. I found myself weeping with him more than once.

At one point, this evangelist asked, "Why did I do it?" His voice broke as he said, "I have asked myself that 10,000 times through 10,000 tears." As I listened, I immediately thought of Psalm 38, which I had been studying. It suddenly seemed like a divine octave, and its melody was being played in this minister's life!

But in truth, we *all* live in the daily reality of the Penitential Psalms.

Recognize the Truth and Necessity of Repentance

The author of Psalm 38 is a believer, probably David himself. He is also a spiritual and political leader of his people. Here he makes himself vulnerable as he describes the state of affairs in his life that resulted from his own personal sin and iniquity.

Perhaps this sin was David's act of adultery with Bathsheba. Remember, that sinful act was followed by deception, hiding, and ultimately the cover-up murder of David's close associate, Uriah — the husband of Bathsheba.

Whether or not David's adulterous relationship with Bathsheba is the specific sin he is referring to, the result of the sin is first conviction and then chastisement. The writer says, "For thine arrows stick fast in me..." (verse 2 *KJV*). This is followed by disorder: "There is no soundness in my flesh..." (verse 3 *KJV*). And, of course, verse 3 (*KJV*) immediately declares, "...neither is there rest in my bones because of my sin."

The psalmist goes on to say, "For my iniquities have gone over my head; like a heavy burden they are too heavy for me. My wounds are foul and festering because of my foolishness" (verses 4,5). Is this is a description of actual physical wounds? The word "wounds" can mean *stripes* and could very well be a reference to the judgment of God upon the writer.

Finally, the psalmist gives expression to his sense of helplessness: "I am feeble and severely broken.... As for the light of my eye, it also has gone from me" (verses 8,10). Could the expression "the light of my eye" refer to the psalmist's creative ability — his brightness, his talent, and his life assignment?

It is all there — the desertion of friends, even of lovers; the careful traps and designs of enemies to destroy him. These words include physical, mental, social, emotional and even spiritual trauma and torment. Some scholars believe that Psalm 38 is the deepest expression in the Bible of the utter prostration that comes to a person's spirit under the severest mental and physical trials, which often come as a result of sin.

The author is rent by a sense of God's displeasure and the related grief of his friends' desertion. Enemies quickly take advantage with their own designs and threats.

It further seems that the psalmist's actual body is smitten with disease. His flesh has no soundness, and his bones are full of aches. His loins are agonized with burning, and his heart is palpitating wildly. Even his eyes are failing him, yet still, he clings to God. He confesses his iniquity; he is genuinely sorry for his sin; and what's more, *he has hope in God!* What a drama!

Alexander MacLaren once wrote concerning this Psalm: "This is a long-drawn wail, passionate at first, but gradually calming itself into submission and trust, although never passing from the minor key."[2] Psalm 38 may be a prayer evoked out of the experience of sickness, with a consequent sense of alienation first from God and eventually from fellow human beings.

One writer is bold enough to suggest that Psalm 38 probably best identifies with the AIDS victims of this particular era.[3] I myself have ministered to people afflicted with AIDS. So often no one will touch them or respond to them, which is reminiscent of the psalmist's words in verse 11. I think this is a very adequate comment that at least we in *our* generation can understand.

Some ancient writers on Psalm 38 believe that the psalmist is describing leprosy, although we certainly don't know of any case of leprosy in David's experience. Perhaps the Psalm is written so we can better understand the potential devastation caused by a disease such as leprosy or AIDS, even though the psalmist himself wasn't actually afflicted with that type of terminal disease.

Finally, it is important to recognize that this Psalm is not spontaneous. It is not a cry of the moment. It is, in fact, highly organized and instructive. Some refer to Psalm 38 as an "alphabetized Psalm," since each two-line unit corresponds to the Hebrew letters in the alphabet. There are also three stanzas, each of which starts with one of the specific Hebrew names of God — either *Elohim, Yahweh,* or *Adonai.*

For you, the important truth is this: Don't read this Psalm as though it has come forth extemporaneously. It has been deliberately written — certainly out of life experience, but also specifically for others' understanding long after the events. You need to know that these words come from deliberation, consideration and life change.

Repentance Is the Believer's Territory

Repentance is the believer's territory! Certainly all Christians ought not to continually live "under the wheel," always feeling as if they have disappointed the Lord and are living in sin. In God's Spirit and grace is the ability to live in victory over the power and damage of sin.

But even with that in mind, the Word of God clearly teaches us in First John 1:8, "If we say that we have no sin, we deceive ourselves, and the truth is not in us." Certainly that scripture is directed to believers. But the text continues, "If we confess our sins, He is faithful and just to forgive us our sins and to cleanse us from all unrighteousness" (1 John 1:9).

Remember, repentance is like exhaling the carbon dioxide — getting rid of what the ancient writers called "stagnant air," eliminating that which is dead out of the system so life can come in. Repentance ought to be as regular as the daily process of washing the dust off our feet. In this case, it is the cleansing of "dust" off our spirits.

Never forget the examples given in the Bible. There is the classic example of Esau who sold his birthright for a little bit of porridge — just a bowl of soup! Hebrews 12:17 says, "For you know that afterward, when he wanted to inherit the blessing, he was rejected, for he found no place for repentance, though he sought it diligently with tears."

Many Christians read that and say, "That's so unfair of God." Not at all! This passage is saying that Esau's repentance was based on what had happened, not on the change of his heart. When he discovered that he had lost material blessing as a result of giving up a spiritual priority, *then* he started weeping.

Esau wasn't crying about the value of his spiritual priority; he was weeping over the loss of material things. God said, "I don't count *that* as true repentance." Surely there is something for each of us to understand in that account about our own motives for repentance.

On the other hand, Peter denied his Lord three times. We can easily see that this was a far more critical issue. Even so, Peter found restoration. He also went out and wept bitterly, but *his* tears were for the right motive. As a result, there was immediate restoration. Peter came through failure with hope.

The book of Joel also talks about repentance. It says to Christians believers, "So rend your hearts, and not your garments..." (Joel 2:13). Now, that may sound strange to you unless you understand the Hebrew customs. During times of repentance, God's people would rip their garments and sit in ashes as a sign of humility and repentance.

Eventually some people decided to rip their garments down the seams so that when the repentance time was over, they could sew them back up again. There is such a difference between real and feigned repentance! The prophet was saying, "Forget this phony stuff. Forget playing games with your relationship with God. Either truly repent from your heart, or just forget it!"

A great Lutheran writer named Erling Olson wrote the following:

It is not unusual for men to be exceeding sorrowful for their sin. The sorrow may be good; and again it may not be good. It may reveal a true heart of repentance, but it could also reveal a heart of stoical indifference. All too frequently men have been sorry that their sin has become known, rather than exhibiting genuine sorrow for their sin. Likewise, men have been sorry for the disastrous results that followed their sin though they did not repent of the sin which in reality was responsible for the results that followed.[4]

The apostle Paul makes a similar contrast:

For even if I made you sorry with my letter, I do not regret it; though I did regret it. For I perceive that the same epistle made you sorry, though only for a while.

Now I rejoice, not that you were made sorry, but that your sorrow led to repentance. For you were made sorry in a godly manner, that you might suffer loss from us in nothing.

For godly sorrow produces repentance leading to salvation, not to be regretted; but the sorrow of the world produces death.

2 Corinthians 7:8-10

Godly sorrow produces diligence, the search to clear oneself, indignation, the fear of God, vehement desire, and zeal (2 Corinthians 7:11). It deals with the true spirit of the issue.

Words like those in Psalm 38 seem almost incredible in this day of "easy believism" and the surpassing emphasis on God's grace. But there is in this Psalm a depth of identity and understanding that ought to speak to us. It must find an octave in our own spirit. We ought to read this in the fear of God, because something in this Psalm is so true of so many of us.

Repentance is our territory, my friend. It is a *daily* experience for those of us who really want to walk in spiritual grace.

Recognize the Opportunity of Your Circumstance

The superscriptions over the Psalms are often considered to be the first verse. Many of these superscriptions are presumed to have been written by the psalmists themselves. In the case of Psalm 38, it says, "To bring to remembrance." This is a very revealing phrase. Only 2 out of all 150 Psalms are introduced with that word "remembrance." It is *zakar* in the Hebrew, meaning "to bring to remembrance."

A key verse of the Old Testament says, "And he appointed certain of the Levites to minister before the ark of the Lord, and *to record, and to thank and praise the Lord God of Israel*" (1 Chronicles 16:4 *KJV*). The *NKJV* reads, "And he appointed some of the Levites to minister before the ark of the Lord, *to commemorate*, to thank, and to praise the Lord God of Israel."

The word "record," or "commemorate" in this scripture is the same word translated "remembrance" in Psalm 38. Earlier in Leviticus 2:2 and Leviticus 24:7, we discover that the meal offering of the tabernacle, a voluntary offering of grain, was twice referred to as a "memorial" offering, which in the literal Hebrew means "the remembrance offering" or "an offering of remembrance."

Without distracting from our principal subject, it is helpful to consider that the word used for the meal offering is never used in reference to the other five offerings. They are all called "sacrifices," or "oblations." But the meal offering is called *minchah*, which is a Hebrew word meaning "a gift offered by an inferior to a superior." *Minchah* is a gift of involvement and ministry. It is a gift of memorializing or remembering.

"How does this apply to me?" you ask. This psalmist is saying, "I'm writing this Psalm as a meal offering to God — not as a blood offering, something demanded or required. I am willingly offering this difficult experience of my life to the Lord so He might receive glory to His own Name through my response to it."

Sand Bags or Bicycles?

The challenge in choosing this response of repentance is to discover the true issues that need to be dealt with in our lives.

There is an amazing story told about the inspectors at the Mexican border. These custom officials must be very cautious because of all the smuggling that goes back and forth over the Mexico-United States border. On this particular day, a young man came riding a bicycle to the border inspection point. The bicycle had two big sacks of sand on either side.

Naturally, the custom officers were suspicious. They took the bags of sand off the bicycle and went through them "with a fine-toothed comb" to see what the teenager was smuggling. In spite of their search, they couldn't find anything but sand! Finally, they put the sacks of sand back on the bike, and the youth crossed over the border.

This young man continued to do the same thing every two weeks for six months. Every time he reached the border, the same scene took place. The customs officers took the sacks off the bicycle and searched through the sand. Then they put the sacks back on the bicycle, and he rode across the border.

Finally the youth stopped coming through. One of the custom guards happened to see him in a local city. The guard went up to him and asked, "Look, I'm off duty, so this has nothing to do with guilt or innocence. Whatever you say, I will not repeat. But you've been driving us crazy! We know you're smuggling something! Tell me, I promise I won't tell anyone. What are you smuggling?"

The boy grinned and simply said, "Bicycles."

Aren't we often like that? We search through "sand bags," looking through the obvious, when *the actual problem is something else entirely*. What may seem obvious often has nothing to do with the real issue God is dealing with us about that requires repentance.

The Difference Is in Our Response

In the same way this writer calls his Psalm a *minchah* — a remembrance or a memorial — to the Lord, we can also respond to God's dealings in *our* lives by willingly offering our own *minchah* — a humble heart of repentance.

Let me relate this story to explain. A husband and wife had a six-month-old baby who died while they were serving as missionaries in Pakistan. A wise old Punjabi heard of their grief and came to comfort them.[5] He told the couple, "A tragedy like this is just being plunged into boiling water. If you are an egg, your affliction will make you hard-boiled and unresponsive. If you are a potato, you will emerge soft, pliable, resilient, and adaptable."

The missionary mother so took those words to her heart that later while writing a book on her experience, she said, "It may sound funny to you, and it may have sounded funny to God, but there have been many times I have prayed since then, 'Oh Lord, please make me like a potato.'"

You see, we are not often made different by the nature of the *crisis;* we become different by the nature of our *response.* We aren't different because some of us are weaker or stronger than most everyone else. We aren't even different because some of us have less or more experience with failure or sin. *We are different by the way we respond to the struggle.*

How people respond determines what times of crisis and suffering will produce in their lives. Some people respond to a crisis in a way that produces bitterness, hardness and resentment. Others allow the same experience to produce brokenness, release and ministry for others. Paul chose the latter response, saying in Second Corinthians 12:10, "...when I am weak, then I am strong."

The Issue of Understanding

Let us acknowledge that the process of repentance is from God Himself. Certainly a major issue of Psalm

38:1-3 is understanding this process. Let me quote these verses from a translation by Dr. Eugene Peterson called *The Message Bible*:[6]

> Take a deep breath, God; calm down — don't be so hasty with your punishing rod.
>
> Your sharp-pointed arrows of rebuke draw blood; my backside smarts from your caning.
>
> I've lost twenty pounds in two months because of your accusation.
>
> My bones are brittle as dry sticks because of my sin.

In verses 3-5 of this Psalm, the psalmist uses three different words as he writes of "his sin": *sin, iniquity,* and *foolishness.* Perhaps the last of these is the most exclamatory word about sin! It is not only transgression, or the breaking of relationship; it is not only iniquity, or "stepping over the line"; and it is not only missing the mark. It is *foolishness!* Yet the psalmist declares, "I receive this as being from You, Lord. I recognize this process is demanding my repentance."

Some Christians are always asking themselves concerning circumstances, "Where did this come from? Is this from the devil, from the flesh, or from God?" But personally, I don't ask that question much anymore. The longer I live, the more I identify with the old Calvinist who fell flat on his face, got up, dusted himself off, and said, "Whoa! I'm glad *that's* over!" In other words, "If that fall was coming, I'm glad it has come and now is over. It is time to get on with my life!"

If this author is David, he seems to be saying, "The *where* question isn't even important. I accept this as an arrow from God." His conclusion isn't affected by whether he was suffering from a disease as a result of his sexual promiscuity, as some have suggested, or describing something other than an actual physical ailment. Emotional struggles can ultimately cause physical problems.

The psalmist's burning loins may refer to ulcers. A palpitating heart may refer to the kind of symptom that happens during any real-life struggle. You may know yourself what it is to awaken in the middle of the night with your heart pounding.

The writer doesn't ponder theology. He simply declares with great honesty, "It is my foolishness, my iniquity, my sin. I understand that, and I receive what's happening as being within the purposes of God."

Perhaps when you and I stop asking the *where* question, we can then start to ask the really mature question — "Why?" "Why am I facing this circumstance in my life, and how am I going to respond to it?" *That's* the issue that counts!

I don't need to worry about how the situation came about or who it came from. The circumstances are here. Since I'm a believer, God has at least permitted them in my life. They have passed through Jesus, for He is the Door of the sheepfold. Nothing comes into my life that hasn't first passed through Jesus!

The psalmist responds, "I accept this as an arrow of God; I accept this as His dealings with me. I'm going to respond to Him in that regard. Lord, it doesn't matter whether it was my sin or my enemies that got me into this mess. The experience is here. You want to do something in my life as a result, and that's what really counts!"

Why do all of us identify so much with David? Why is the book of Psalms the only book held sacred by Muslims, Jews, and Christians alike? Why is it that in our need we often go to the Psalms?

I think I know the answer. Men and women in the Psalms have opened up their spirits to us during God's dealings in the difficult circumstances of their lives. Those difficult circumstances were redeemed when they turned their experience over to God. We identify with the vulnerable honesty of that process.

Some Christians in such circumstances rationalize and try to justify themselves, hiding from their sin and playing games with God. Naturally, no one who responds this way ever receives the brokenness that could make him whole and give him the vulnerability needed to open up his life to another brother or sister in the Lord.

A major theme in Alcoholics Anonymous is that "You are only as sick as your secrets." Repentance is meant to penetrate the crusts of piety and the excuses believers wrap around themselves in order to keep from changing. People who internalize and hide deep spiritual or moral secrets are left in emotional and often physical pain.

Repentance begins inside the heart. It turns our lives upside down for us, but right side up for God. Do you see this? The secrets the Holy Spirit reveals so they can be dealt with may be secrets even to us, buried deeply in our subconscious mind.

Donald Williams, a Presbyterian pastor and an adjunct faculty member at a leading United States seminary, writes of some the secrets hidden deep within so many people:

Some excessively dependent adults may be seeking in their relationships the parental love they failed to receive as children. Or, confusing approval for love, some spend their lives working for approval but come up empty handed so far as love is concerned. Repressed anger toward parents, which we are afraid to admit for fear of losing their love, may be the cause of chronic depression. Then there are conscious secrets: sexual sin, consuming jealousy, self-protecting lies, and spiritual hypocrisy.[7]

Could you accept the premise that Psalm 38 is in the Bible to help each of us bring these secrets to light? God wants to break the chains off our lives so He can start us on the road to true healing. Repentance shatters all our systems of security and hangs us on the thin thread we often call the will of God.

This psalmist is a man holding on to God by such a thread. Yet as he bares his soul, he begins to take vulnerable steps toward healing. These steps can also be healing and effective therapy to each reader.

Repentance *reverses our priorities, upsets our values, and turns our pockets inside out.* As we honestly study this Psalm of penitence, there is great potential for the deepest places in our lives to be opened and made whole.

Perhaps we should ask ourselves the age-old question, "If this were the last day of my life, what would I do with it?" The truest answer to that question could only come on our knees. Humbly and with head bowed, we need to listen for an answer from the very throne of God! God's answers are not unjustly punitive, but they may very well provide the discipline of a loving Father.

The Relinquishment of Self-Defense

In the second stanza of Psalm 38, the psalmist recognizes that the real issue for every person is God's omniscience. God really knows what is going on! This, of course, reveals the ultimate issue of trust and the final issue of faith — *the relinquishment of self-defense.*

The psalmist begins in verse 9 by saying, "Lord, all my desire is before You; and my sighing is not hidden from You." The Hebrew suggests an even deeper paraphrase: "You're the only One who delights me, the only One I'm really satisfied with." Here the psalmist recognizes that what's happening in him spiritually is more important than anything else. That's the entire purpose of this Psalm. That's where this is all going!

It is in this portion of Psalm 38 that the writer talks about companions who won't even touch him because of his plague: "My loved ones and my friends stand aloof from my plague, and my relatives stand afar off" (verse 11). Interesting, isn't it? All of us know that this can happen as a result of any revelation of our weaknesses. As I have previously mentioned, one commentator, Donald Williams, writes regarding this verse: "David experiences the abandonment that many AIDS victims receive today. No one wants to be near him or to touch him."[8]

The next verse of this stanza, verse 12, speaks of the psalmist's enemies getting involved to take advantage of him. I'm sure the American evangelist I mentioned earlier could identify with this verse. He must have quickly discovered that there were people after him he didn't even know about!

I believe a spirit of divisiveness and "neo-legalism" has been released into the evangelical world through these types of people. I speak against that spirit in the Name of the Lord!

The minister I mentioned had been greatly used of God to bless people around the world. During the traumatic time when he fell morally, I wonder if as many Christians were praying for his moral success as satanic people were praying for his moral failure! It is a valid question, isn't it?

In essence, David is saying in verse 11, "My friends withdraw from me; my lovers stand aloof from me; my kinsmen and neighbors stand afar off. No one wants to touch me; no one even wants to be involved with me." Then in verses 13 and 14, the psalmist writes, "But I, like a deaf man, do not hear; and I am like a mute who does not open his mouth. Thus I am like a man who does not hear, and in whose mouth is no response."

Does this sound odd to you? David started this stanza by saying, "Lord, all my desire is before You..." (verse 9), and now he ends it by basically saying, "I am not going to justify myself or argue with anyone; there is no reproof in my mouth. I'm just going to lay my case before the Lord."

Perhaps this is the ultimate issue — trust! Isn't it interesting to hear us try to explain things when something goes wrong? Some of us talk a mile a minute: "But, you see, the problem was this, and this, and this, and if that and that had only happened..." You know what I mean. It can be really funny — almost hilarious! By way of contrast, what a place of ultimate trust has been attained when we can say, "I have nothing to say."

When scandals expose the weakness of Christian leaders, the ultimate issue to the world as it watches is "What is the church like?" In other words, people are wondering, "Can you come to church with your hurts and your needs? Is the church a safe place?"

How important it is that our brothers and sisters in Christ are a place of refuge, confidence, and safety! Unfortunately, when Christian failure is much publicized and exposed, the reaction in the church is often just the opposite! In the process of exposure, a spirit of withdrawal enters many Christian hearts.

I really think that's the "bicycle" being smuggled into the Body of Christ. The issue seems to be morality and sin, but Satan's real goal is to produce a sense of withdrawal and a fear of being honest with one another. He wants to keep us too afraid to expose our needs and our hearts to each other.

Unfortunately, during a recent crisis of this nature, almost every time a news reporter shoved a microphone in a preacher's face, the preacher would reply, "Well, I can tell you some things you don't know yet. Let me tell you some other things I know about."

Imagine the difference in this scenario: A prominent Christian leader falls into sin, and the microphones of the world are turned on the church. But when news reporters stick a microphone in Christians' faces and ask, "What do you have to say about this crisis?" the reporters receive only one response: "Well, let's not talk about his sin. If you want to talk about sin, let me talk about mine. Let me tell you about me. Let me tell you about the fact that, except for the grace and mercy of God, this is who I am. Let me talk about what reconciliation means in the Bible. If you want to talk to me, if you want to give me some air time, let me talk about grace. Let me talk about what God does in the lives of common, weak, and sinful people!"

Wouldn't that be phenomenal? Instead of judgment, the message of the Church would become reconciliation! We'd be given all that air time to share the message of God's grace, and we wouldn't have to spend a dime to buy it! Now, *that* would turn the tables on the enemy!

When faced with rejecting friends, snickering neighbors and scheming enemies, David's response is "I will not respond — I am silent before my accusers." Let me strongly suggest a reason for that response.

Could any possible good have resulted if David had attempted to gain a hearing? God speedily undertakes the cause of those who quietly and patiently leave everything in His hands. Such meekness in the midst of urgent need calls out loudly for divine intervention.

Certainly the psalmist's consciousness of his sin also leaves him obliged to be silent. But I believe an overriding truth lies behind his words: trust and commitment to the omniscience of God. He is saying, "God thoroughly knows me; He knows my end from my beginning. He chose me, even knowing all my potential for both good and evil. God don't make no junk! Therefore, I trust my affairs, including my weaknesses, to His understanding, grace and redemption."

Expectation and Hope

How quickly things change in Psalm 38! "For in You, O Lord, I hope; you will hear, O Lord my God" (verse 15). The Hebrew word for "hope" here is *yachal*, which means "to wait, to hope, to expect, to be patient, to tarry." The psalmist has recognized a key point: The source of an answer to his problems lies in some kind of action from the Lord.

This closing stanza is equally filled with fearful potentials. His enemies may still rejoice and magnify themselves over him when his foot slips (verse 16). He admits, "…I am ready to fall, and my sorrow is continually before me. For I will declare my iniquity; I will be in anguish over my sin" (verses 17,18).

The psalmist's enemies are vigorous and strong. In fact, people who hate him wrongfully are actually multiplying! Others are rendering evil for the good he has done, and another group opposes him not for his sin, but

for his choice to "follow what is good." It is obvious —
he just can't win.

I personally believe we need to read this stanza
backward, or at least repeat verse 15 after verse 20. It is,
after all, the faith statement of the Psalm: "I wait for You,
Lord. You are my expectation." This word *yachal* is used
36 times in the Old Testament (Genesis 8:12; 1 Samuel
13:8; Job 14:14.) It often implies waiting for the passage
of time. (By the way, this one verse, verse 15, uses all
three Hebrew names of God: *Jehovah, Adonai,* and *Elohim.*

Within the waiting are the strongest terms of repentance, sorrow, and even acceptance of results. The
psalmist says, "I'm prepared for limping; I know there
will be consequences for my sin." But here again is ultimate faith and the true, intimate knowledge of the ways
of God. "The God I believe in will hear me," he writes.
"He will redeem my circumstance; He will in fact inter-
vene. That's my true expectation." The writer isn't
focused on all the in-between results, but on the ultimate
revelation. "God will show up, and I will be glad!"

Saving Faith

This entire study reveals that repentance is not only
important, but a prerequisite for a relationship with God.
But as is always preached in the New Testament, the
Gospel has a two-edged sword: repentance toward God
and faith in the Lord Jesus Christ.

I never underestimate the need for a genuine, specific
sorrow for sin. But that godly sorrow must be considered
as preliminary — never the means of a solution. I could
be sorry for my sins for eternity, but that sorrow in itself
would never save me. Only one thing saves any of us,

and that is the sacrifice of our Lord Jesus Christ. His blood makes atonement for the soul — once and for all!

The psalmist cries out in conclusion, "Do not forsake me, O Lord; O my God, be not far from me! Make haste to help me, O Lord, my salvation!" (Psalm 38:21,22). In one new translation, that final expression reads, "O Lord, my Victory!"

The word "salvation" is the Hebrew word *shaua*, which means "help, assistance, deliverance, welfare and salvation." It refers primarily to God's acts of help and rescue that have already occurred and have been experienced. I do not exaggerate this word's meaning when I say it means "to be free; to get the help needed to break free from some trouble."

This is the Gospel in the hands of a vulnerable writer. I frequently quote the words of one hymn:

> *Nothing in my hand I bring,*
> *Simply to Thy cross I cling;*
> *Naked, come to Thee for dress,*
> *Helpless, look to Thee for grace;*
> *Foul, I to the fountain fly,*
> *Wash me, Saviour, or I die!*[9]

Those lyrics speak of David. At various times in his life, he faced failure, sin, enemies and disease — consequences both deserved and undeserved. But he maintained the attitude, "It is all in God's hands. I repent; I turn; I renounce; I feel sorrow."

We, too, face negative consequences in our lives, both deserved and undeserved. But it is the application of our Lord's blood shed on Calvary that delivers us. That is the fountain to which we fly. Thank God, it is available to all who want to be clean.

Lord, You are our Victory. You free us. Hallelujah!

PSALM 51

Fourth of the Penitential Psalms

How we long for renewal! Every area of our life is so easily corroded and stained. Our marriages need renewal. As Scot Peck observes we must fall in love again and again. Our families need renewal. It is tragic that often it takes illness or death to reunite us. Our churches need renewal when liturgy becomes mechanical, the prayers rote, and programs perfunctory. But most of all, we need personal renewal — deep inner conviction of our own sin and poverty — followed by a fresh cleansing and infilling of God's Spirit.

There is no renewal apart from pain. This pain may come in moral crisis. It may come when the placid order of life is broken by illness, economic reversal, or an upheaval in relationships. It may come when we reflect upon the pace with which life passes and upon our haunting need for meaning. Carl Jung said that all of the people over forty years old coming to see him for psychiatric help were looking for some reason to continue living.[1]

— Donald M. Williams
The Communicator's Commentary

CHAPTER 4

The Perfect Prayer for Renewal

Psalm 51

$\mathcal{P}$SALM 51

To the chief musician. A Psalm of David, when Nathan the prophet went to him after he had gone into Bathsheba.

Have mercy upon me, O God, according to Your lovingkindness; according to the multitude of Your tender mercies, blot out my transgressions.

Wash me thoroughly from my iniquity, and cleanse me from my sin.

For I acknowledge my transgressions, and my sin is always before me.

Against You, You only, have I sinned, and done this evil in Your sight— that You may be found just when You speak, and blameless when You judge.

Behold, I was brought forth in iniquity, and in sin my mother conceived me.

Behold, You desire truth in the inward parts, and in the hidden part You will make me to know wisdom.

Purge me with hyssop, and I shall be clean; wash me, and I shall be whiter than snow.

Make me to hear joy and gladness, that the bones You have broken may rejoice.

Hide Your face from my sins, and blot out all my iniquities.

Create in me a clean heart, O God, and renew a steadfast spirit within me.

Do not cast me away from Your presence, and do not take Your Holy Spirit from me.

Restore to me the joy of Your salvation, and uphold me by Your generous Spirit.

Then I will teach transgressors Your ways, and sinners shall be converted to You.

Deliver me from the guilt of bloodshed, O God, the God of my salvation, and my tongue shall sing aloud of Your righteousness.

O Lord, open my lips, and my mouth shall show forth Your praise.

For You do not desire sacrifice, or else I would give it; you do not delight in burnt offering.

The sacrifices of God are a broken spirit, a broken and a contrite heart — these, O God, You will not despise.

Do good in Your good pleasure to Zion; build the walls of Jerusalem.

Then You shall be pleased with the sacrifices of righteousness, with burnt offering and whole burnt offering; then they shall offer bulls on Your altar.

Repentance is never about human resolution. That is always *so* inadequate. There is a very wide difference between a mere *resolution* to change and true commitment.

What we must have is *divine revolution*! Certainly wishful thinking won't do. We must have transformed minds. The breath of God must stir among us.

All of mankind truly hungers for the reality of God's presence in their lives. People long for an invigorating move of God within their spirits that is both rarified and invigorating. But before such renewal is possible, there has to be repentance. That's why the topic of this book is so important. We must all learn to live in the spirit of grace and repentance.

Ever since the second century, Christians have used the seven Penitential Psalms as a way to identify uniquely with Christ in His denial of self and His sufferings. So never become overwhelmed by the concept of repentance. Respond only to the Holy Spirit. *Know that conviction is not condemnation!* If you are one of those who desires a new work of the Holy Spirit in your life, recognize that there will always be a preparation in your own spirit that will include *repentance.*

The Best-Known Psalm of Penitence

The world's best known Penitential Psalm is Psalm 51. It is also the very first Psalm in which the word "Spirit" is used in connection with the Holy Spirit. Of all inspired Scripture, the 51st Psalm is perhaps second only to the Lord's prayer as the most often repeated passage of Scripture by the Church. In fact, for 1,300 years in the Christian church, it was repeated seven times daily, except on the great feast days. Luther wrote, "There is no other Psalm which is more often sung or prayed in the church."[2]

Commentator Donald Williams writes, "As we study this prayer, we are at one of the deepest levels of Bible revelation." Then he adds, "We must prepare to be changed."[3] Indeed, Psalm 51 is one of the deepest levels of biblical understanding. Referring to this psalm, many writers suggest, "When you read it, you've got to get ready because the Spirit wants to do something to change your life."

Psalm 51 is really a positive Psalm! The great Austrian composer, Franz Joseph Haydn, understood this. He was once asked, "Why is all of your sacred music so joyful?" Haydn replied that it was because God was so good that He would even set the 51st Psalm in Allegro![3]

Allegro is a musical term that means "brisk"; "performed fast"; or "spirited and cheerful." Although Psalm 51 ultimately concerns God's dealings in the midst of dark circumstances, yet it is indeed a record of spirited, grace-filled life.

Start at the Beginning

Psalm 51 has 19 dynamic verses that we will review in the course of this chapter. The superscription or introductory phrase of Psalm 51 reads, "To the chief musician, a Psalm of David, when Nathan the prophet went to him after he had gone into Bathsheba." Now, that's plenty specific!

There are, of course, some commentators who have questions about whether or not this Psalm was written by David. They object on two grounds. First, in verse 4 the psalmist writes, "Against You, You only, have I sinned...."

"How could that be?" the commentators ask. "The sin was really against Bathsheba and Uriah and against the people of God that David was leading."

Personally, I don't believe that is the point. David was not denying his sin against those he led into sin, nor those specifically affected by his wrongful action. He *was* recognizing, however, that the ultimate direction of all rebellion is against the throne of authority, which is the throne of God. All sin is ultimately *against* God.

The second objection to David's authorship is found in the latter two verses where the "wall of Jerusalem" is mentioned. "There were no walls in Jerusalem under David," critics say. "Therefore, Psalm 51 must have come at a later time."

I think this misses the point entirely. David isn't writing about literal walls. Indeed, several times in the Old Testament, the people of Israel referred to the strength of the Lord Jehovah as their tower and protection. The reconstruction of Zion fits beautifully in David's time and doesn't have to refer to either the cessation of sacrifices, nor to the physical walls of Jerusalem.

Obviously, I believe David wrote Psalm 51. I believe he wrote it exactly at the time the superscription says he did — when he was confronted by Nathan, his own brother in faith.

David and Nathan had been Bible school roommates under Samuel; one trained to be a prophet, and the other to be a theocratic king. God always wants to remind us that "as iron sharpens iron, so a man sharpens the countenance of his friend" (Proverbs 27:17).

David was a king with the potential fury of the oriental despot. But in that moment of confrontation, he yielded to the truth and cried out to Nathan, "...I have sinned against the Lord..." (2 Samuel 12:13).

The following quote has been in my notes for many years. I have always attributed it to the great English preacher, Alexander MacLaren. Although I do not have specific source information on the quote, I include it because the words express an imperative understanding:

A saint of nearly 50 years of age, bound to God by ties which he rapturously felt and acknowledged, whose words have been the very breath of devotion for every devout heart, forgets his **longings** after righteousness; flings away the joys of divine communion; darkens his soul; ends his prosperity; brings down upon his head for all his remaining years a cataract of calamities; and makes his name and religion a target for the barbed sarcasm of each succeeding generation of scoffers. As a man; as king; as soldier — he is found wanting. Why should we dwell on this wretched story, *except that it teaches, as no other page in the history of God's church does that the alchemy of Divine Love can extract sweet perfume of penitence and praise out of the filth of sin* (italics my own).

Who confesses sin? Only believers confess sin. The unbeliever isn't saved by the confession of sin. He can only come to God to claim the righteousness of Christ — *period.*

Believers confess sin. But this doesn't actually refer to "asking" the Lord for forgiveness. Those are two totally different procedures! God can do nothing else about forgiveness. The sacrifice of Jesus Christ has already put away sin through the offering of His blood.

But God does ask that we confess or agree with the way He sees our sin. That's why First John 1:9 applies only to believers: "If we confess our sins, He is faithful and just to forgive us our sins, and to cleanse us from all unrighteousness."

Repentance is uniquely the believer's territory. Christians certainly don't live without sin. Yet when a person becomes a believer, he is more conscious of sin than ever before. Is that not true? The white light of the Holy Spirit makes the believer aware of motives and attitudes far deeper than just actions — and, thus, the need for repentance.

Again let me refer to our oft-repeated analogy: Repentance is exhaling the old, stagnant air and breathing in the new, oxygen-rich provision of God. This must be a daily part of life if we are going to be happy as believers. We desperately need consistent renewal. We need renewal in our marriages and in our families. We need a fresh cleansing that keeps action from becoming perfunctory and work-oriented, religious and ritualistic.

Karl Jung, the great psychologist, reportedly said that all the over-40 people who came to see him for psychiatric help were actually looking for some reason to continue living! We as Christians are not immune to this state of mind. That's why renewal is a very strategic part of what it means for us to be believers — not just obtaining forgiveness or dealing with some notorious issue or sin in which we have failed the Lord. The *true* issue is our need for renewal.

Re-vival means a restoration of life! Unbelievers are spiritually dead, so they need "vival," not *re*-vival! Believers are the ones who need revival — a restoration of life.

An Overview of Psalm 51

Psalm 51 has an interesting organization of four stanzas, including the conclusion. The first stanza has four verses that are a cry for repentance; the second stanza is about restoration and cleansing. The third stanza tells what the results of this cleansing will be and how they will manifest in practical life. Finally, there is a two-verse projection of concern for Zion as a whole. (I believe any true believer's experience of repentance includes specific concern about God's collective purpose among His people. Every believer affects the entire Body of Christ.)

More than any of the other 150 Psalms, Psalm 51 needs to be extensively discussed in a book and not just in a small chapter. There are lists of entire books written on the 51st Psalm. Martin Luther, for example, wrote a large section on it. The reason is obvious. Psalm 51 is so eclectic — so diverse in what it covers. It touches on many crucial theological issues, such as the depravity of human nature.

For our brief purpose, however, let me list four basic issues contained within the Psalm. First, we will look at the actual prayer for forgiveness. This section speaks of the reality and nature of sin, as well as its direction and ultimate depths.

The Direction of Man's Sin

In this first section, David makes strong statements about his understanding of sin's nature. As we have seen before, David consistently uses three words for sin: *transgression*, which implies a rebellion against a relationship; *iniquity*, which implies something crooked thrown down against the straight law of God; and, finally, *sin*, which means to miss the mark and to come short of God's glory and of His purpose for one's life.

In the 38th Psalm, David added the word "foolishness." Indeed, all sin *is* foolishness! In Psalm 51, he adds the words "blood guiltiness." Let your spirit record this important truth: Even the blood of Jesus Christ cannot erase the scars of sin in a life.

David also uses the word "evil" in this Psalm, a word that means "that which spoils and breaks something to pieces." To summarize, he uses *sin*, *transgression*, *iniquity*, *foolishness*, *blood guiltiness* and *evil*. What a powerful summary of sin's nature is contained in those words!

But David not only talks of the *nature* of sin; he also adds the issue of sin's *direction*. No more important understanding may exist in the Bible than verse 4:

"Against *You, You only* have I sinned and done this evil in Your sight.."

Perhaps there is no true repentance until we understand that our saying, "I repent" can really mean "I'm sorry I was caught" or "I'm scared of the punishment I'll get if I don't repent!" God is not seeking this type of ritualistic repentance. He desires repentance that comes from acknowledging the brokenness sin has caused at the throne of God. That is certainly David's understanding of sin's direction!

Although Uriah's life was taken and Bathsheba's life was dramatically changed because of David's sin, let us never think that this was David's only sin or his ultimate focus. David admits that the real issue, the ultimate direction of sin in his life, is against the authority of God.

The Depths of Man's Sin

In this same stanza, David further speaks about the depths of this sin. It is a controversial verse but an important one to understand: "Behold, I was brought forth in iniquity, And in sin my mother conceived me."

Could this suggest that David was an illegitimate child? I don't believe so. In at least two other Old Testament scriptures, David writes specifically about the integrity of his mother's character (Psalm 86:16; 116:16). In reality, I believe David is talking about the difference between specific *sins* and the *sin nature* — between the sins man chooses to commit and the fallen nature of humans to practice unrighteousness.

We were all born rebellious. Even the smallest child demands his own way. This is the ultimate expression of unrighteousness — demanding and going our own way (Isaiah 53:6).

I love to include the children in every Sunday morning worship service. They come up and sit with me near the platform, and I share an inspirational truth, usually with an illustration and occasionally a small gift for them.

When I look at these clean-faced children, I realize they have not been trained in "graduate-level" rebellion. What selfishness and egocentricity they possess has come automatically. Do you understand the difference? Children were born with a Ph.D. in rebellion!

When we understand the depths of sin, we better understand the nature and totality of Calvary. When Christ died, He didn't just deal with the "muck-up" that people make of their lives. He dealt with the very nature of rebellion that originated with Lucifer and was passed on from Adam and Eve to every person born on this earth. Some nice little religious formula wasn't going to provide the solution — it would take a radical work of God. *The nature of sin requires the depth of God's radical redemption at Calvary!*

Prayer for Forgiveness

But Psalm 51 declares also the nature of forgiveness: "Have mercy upon me, O God, according to Your lovingkindness; according to the multitude of Your tender mercies, blot out my transgressions. Wash me thoroughly from my iniquity, and cleanse me from my sin" (Psalm 51:1,2).

Three verbs are used here to express what needs to happen. First, David asks the Lord to "blot out" his transgression. This means God won't keep the debt on the ledger anymore! That's what instantaneous justification by faith is all about. When by faith a person believes in Jesus Christ, the ledger of his sins is blotted out for eternity, never to be remembered against him again. Praise God!

But David also uses a "laundry" verb, asking God to "wash" him of his sin. Further, he cries, "Cleanse me!" The word "cleanse" in the Hebrew means "to smelt precious metal; to put fire on until only the pure rises to the top." David is saying, "I really need a radical work done. It isn't just enough that You, O God, are satisfied or that You have hidden my transgression. Something needs to change *inside me*. I want to be refined; I want to be smelted."

Of course, such a blotting, washing, and cleansing can only be done on the basis of three attributes of God's very character: His *mercy*, His *lovingkindness*, and His *tender mercies*. Those three attributes describe three waves of order in God's own person.

The first attribute, "mercy," describes a superior who stoops down to be kind to an inferior. And upon what is mercy truly based? The answer is "lovingkindness." This word means "covenant love," *not* performance. David is saying, "Lord, I don't want You to be merciful because I am promising never to fail again for the rest of my life."

How many times do we say, "I promise I will never do that again, God"? David doesn't make that mistake. He understands his nature: "God, be merciful to me on the basis that *You* keep the covenants You make. The renewal of Your love for me is based on Your loyal covenant-keeping commitment."

The third attribute, "tender mercies," is a feminine description. In the Scriptures, God is often described as possessing the deep mothering qualities we all identify with, although He ever remains Father God. The original language that implies God's maternal characteristics is very clear throughout the Old Testament. Even in the New Testament, Paul is not afraid to say, "But we were gentle among you, just as a nursing mother cherishes her own children" (1 Thessalonians 2:7). Obviously, Paul had enough self-identity to boldly proclaim such an imperative role for his ministry!

Tender mercies speaks of a mother's absolute, unalterable love for her child. It includes the concept of parental sympathy or "bowels of compassion." It is as though David is saying, "Look, when You forgive me, Lord, don't only do it because You're a superior who stoops down to minister to me. Don't only do it because You and I have a covenant. I want you to forgive me out of a parental love that comes from You toward me."

Ah, friend, if you come to God with any less expectation than that, you are missing it! Never think that God blots out your sin and says, "But don't do it again, turkey, or you're finished! Three strikes and you're *out!*" *That could never be the character of God.*

Psalm 51 rings with glorious statements of God's character. This opening stanza describes His compassion, His longsuffering and His mercy. God is the righteous Judge, yet He is also forever committed to us as our loving Parent.

The Petition for Holiness

David now pleads for a basic change in his entire nature — who he is in his own inner person.

Purge me with hyssop, and I shall be clean; wash me, and I shall be whiter than snow.

Make me to hear joy and gladness, that the bones You have broken may rejoice.

Hide Your face from my sins, and blot out all my iniquities.

Psalm 51:7-9

The verb for "purge" could just as easily be translated *"un-sin* me." The illustration David has in mind seems to be the rite of purification for a leper's house (Leviticus 14:52). However, hyssop spread with blood was also used on the door posts of the Hebrew homes during the Passover. This deep cleaning that David boldly seeks is that of a total restoration. As Isaiah later wrote, "Though your sins are like scarlet, they shall be as white as snow" (Isaiah 1:18).

With this restoration comes a new understanding of true joy: "Make me to hear joy and gladness, that the bones You have broken may rejoice" (verse 8).

How sad to be forgiven and not changed — to experience grace without intense learning! David not only wants cleansing; he wants renewed communion with God. Why endure chastisement without learning, or suffering without renewed obedience? David's desire for holiness isn't only to be changed but to have his very process of repentance redeemed by God. David wants to once again hear the voice of God in his intimate inner life!

David writes about that restored intimacy in verse 9, asking God to work this work in him: "Hide Your face from my sins, and blot out all my iniquities" (Psalm 51:9). This is the beginning of a cry for restored intimacy. David is saying, "God, I can believe that You will forgive me. I can believe that You will declare me righteous. I thank You that even now, my house is once again in order by Your Name. But the most difficult thing for me to believe is that You'll ever let me become intimate with You again the way I was before."

Some of us don't believe that is possible. Our very language declares, "I know God forgives me, but it will never be the same again! I've blown it. God will never give me another opportunity to be where I was before. I missed the will of God here and there, and I just know it can never be the same." Please understand that *this is an entirely wrong understanding of God's character*! God not only forgives and declares to the world that we are now clean and ready, but He says, "Come again into the intimacy you had with Me before."

Listen again to David's understanding: "Create in me a clean heart, O God, and renew a steadfast spirit within me. Do not cast me away from Your presence, and do not take Your Holy Spirit from me" (Psalm 51:11).

When David prays in verse 10, "Create in me a clean heart...," he is using the Hebrew word *bara*, the same word for "create" used in Genesis 1 for the creation of the universe. *"Bara,"* he says. "God, out of nothing, make something!" *David is asking for a radical newness in his life.*

Why ask God to forgive your sins if you don't want to be different? If you want to keep blundering around in the same old sin, why ask God to forgive you? You must set a new target — something radical and wonderful — as your hope for the future. Tell the Lord, "O God, I want new life! Create out of nothing something wonderful, just as You did in the original creation."

The Promise of Service

Please don't miss the importance of the next stanza in Psalm 51:12-17.

Restore to me the joy of Your salvation, and uphold me by Your generous Spirit.

101

Then I will teach transgressors Your ways, and sinners shall be converted to You.

Deliver me from bloodshed, O God, the God of my salvation, and my tongue shall sing aloud of Your righteousness.

O Lord, open my lips, and my mouth shall show forth Your praise.

For You do not desire sacrifice, or else I would give it; you do not delight in burnt offering.

The sacrifices of God are a broken spirit, a broken and a contrite heart — these, O God, You will not despise.

Here David prays that, out of his experience of failure, he would become a *credible witness*. He believes that he will be able to teach unbelievers and transgressors the ways of God. He also sees his experience as an acceptable sacrifice from his life, now that he has surrendered it to God.

David talks of *singing aloud*, a phrase that actually implies a ringing cry or shout. God's righteousness will now be trumpeted in David's life! What's more, he can now come before God with the correct sacrifice — a broken and contrite spirit.

Donald Williams writes, "Credible witness comes from those whose lives have been redeemed from their own hell. Paul can deal so effectively with legalism because he was a legalist, (Philippians 3:2 ff.). When we witness from our own wounds, the world can identify with us. Also, when we witness from our wounds, the glory goes to God and not to us."[4]

A Corporate Result

Finally, in David's renewed understanding, he believes that a corporate good will result from what has happened in his life. A renewed strength will come to the very character of Jerusalem through his own revival: "Do good in Your good pleasure to Zion; build the walls of Jerusalem" (verse 18).

One preacher I know frequently tells pastors in his ministry that if he were the devil, he would do two things to the Church: 1) Discourage the leaders, and 2) Divide the Body. Can we understand this last truth of David's renewed understanding? *A renewed leader will always renew the people.* The people of "Zion" will be blessed through the blessing of their spiritual leadership.

It's important that we recognize and care about that corporate blessing. We live in such an individualized culture. Our motto is too often "Jesus and me on the Jericho Road" or "There's room for just two, just Jesus and you."

I think it is fair to doubt the reality of anybody's experience of repentance who doesn't also expect a corporate result to that experience. I doubt that God wants to do anything in anyone's life that doesn't reflect on the good of the Church.

God makes us whole. He heals and teaches us, placing those of us who are solitary in families, or local churches. He does this in order to provide a reflection of what He has done for one in the *celebration of the Body.* Thus, David's prayer still applies today: "O God, build the walls of Jerusalem."

Are We Seeing?

So much emerges from this Psalm to speak to us in a very specific way. Augustine, the great Early Church father, wrote: "If there is one madness greater than another, it is this, — not to be ashamed of the wound, but to be ashamed of the bandage."[5]

It seems to me that Psalm 51 is not just a spontaneous and emotional outpouring from David's encounter with Nathan. It is much more logical than that. Hidden in this Psalm are some critical truths we all need to know in order to understand repentance and grace. The following are some of the conclusions that have been the most revealing to me in the study of Psalm 51.

First, our Father is seeking people who will internalize truth — people who seize truth not simply for the pragmatic reason of changing their circumstances, but also to satisfy a deeper level of inner reality. David writes, "Behold, You desire truth in the inward parts, and in the hidden part You will make me to know wisdom" (Psalm 51:6).

As a whole, we are all very external in our responses. Seldom do we allow ourselves any vulnerable relationships. We not only build fences around our homes, but too often we build fences around our spirits, or hearts. Few, if any, people know the areas in which we individually struggle or where our greatest weaknesses or problems lie. Thus, if we ever give in to our weaknesses, our failure shocks even the people who are closest to us. They thought they knew us!

Why is that? Perhaps because we are so externalized in our society. We change our eyeglasses — not because we need a new prescription, but because the frames are no longer popular. We dress with the utmost concern. Fashion designers become lords of our culture. Even much of our religious response is external. We say, "Well, it just didn't move me today. I suppose the message was okay, but, you know, I just don't *feel* anything!"

Our entire American society is based on "spectating" — sitting on the edge of the seat and being entertained. It is pretty hard to believe in a God who says, "I want to know what you're like on the inside. I want to know what truth lies deep within you."

Indeed, deep within our spirits is where truth is *supposed* to be! That is where we are going to learn. I have always desired the fellowship of a church that would reflect that kind of integrity and vulnerability. God help us to base truth on something other than the external!

David really found something out about God through this experience. He paid a steep price, but he found out that God wanted to relate to him in his spirit, deep within his inner self!

Second, David expressed a very dramatic truth in verse 8: "Make me to hear joy and gladness, that the bones You have broken may rejoice." At 50-plus years of age, David was saying, "I don't want to live one remaining day of my life affected by the limitations of this sin. I expect a healing to come to my spirit regarding the issues of chastisement and judgment in which God righteously administers judgment to my life."

What's more, David expected a *total* healing. He expected to become a whole person. This second major understanding I have just reviewed is how the result of release is often brought to pass through the process of wounding and healing.

In order to be healed, believers must be willing to discard their "crutches" — the limitations of the sins and weaknesses they have nurtured for too long. However, many are *not* willing. Just listen to how people talk, and you will detect those who want to hang on to their invisible crutches.

"How are you doing?" we ask.

"All right," comes the reply, "under the circumstances."

"How's everything going with you?"

"Well, it hasn't been a very good week."

Often we know the response before we ask the question! "How are you feeling?"

"Well, my bursitis, you know."

My dad used to tell about a woman who was a hypochondriac. Just before this woman finally died, she had an inscription written on her tombstone that said, "I told you I was sick!"

Do you need *your* crutches? Even the results of God's chastisement in your life are not meant to be crutches that keep you limping for the rest of your time on this earth. You are not to abstain from sin only because of the threat of some phenomenal, crippling consequence should you yield to it!

David was saying, "God, I expect total restoration. The very bones You have broken will be healed. I'll be made to rejoice." That's what I call faith!

Let us all commit to responding to the last years of our lives in a brilliant, blazing worship of Almighty God! May every circumstance be redeemed for the purposes of God. *Why must we live as emotional and spiritual cripples when God wants us whole?*

Making Your Experience Count

Along with his desire for healing, David also desired a restored anointing and a true spiritual renewal: "Create [*bara*] in me a clean heart, O God, and renew a steadfast spirit within me" (Psalm 51:10). This is a phenomenal thing David was praying for. He was asking that through God's redemption of all the circumstances of his life, a profound release of newness would produce greater anointing and multiplied ministry!

I guess I've never known anyone anointed who had not paid a price for it. When I hear people say, "I'd like to have a ministry like yours," I often cringe! Wherever someone exhibits a great anointing or release in his ministry, you can know that a price has been paid in that life.

But the reverse is also true. Don't waste your sufferings! Don't waste the dealings and chastisement of God in your life! These become the foundation of renewed ministry.

David writes that after this experience of repentance and renewal, he will "...teach transgressors Your ways, and sinners shall be converted to You" (Psalm 51:13). What a statement of faith!

This is released ministry through the redemption of circumstances. *That's how you make your experience count.*

The Sacrifice That God Esteems

I received a final jolt in my dealings with Psalm 51 when I studied verses 16 and 17: "For You do not desire sacrifice, or else I would give it; you do not delight in burnt offering. The sacrifices of God are a broken spirit, a broken and a contrite heart — these, O God, You will not despise."

David speaks here of a revitalized and realized true worship. We must realize that this was an era dependent on animal sacrifices in worship. Animals were killed both for the atonement of sin and for voluntary service offerings. That makes David's words a radical declaration!

Perhaps the priests were out in front of the palace the next day saying, "We protest a king who doesn't believe in our burnt offerings!" Can you imagine? It would be like a pastor standing behind the pulpit and saying, "I don't believe God wants us to have church next Sunday." That *would* be interesting, wouldn't it?

David was saying, "What God has always wanted is a broken spirit and a contrite heart. He will never despise someone who comes with this as his offering. It really doesn't matter what is in a person's hands; it's what is in his *spirit* that counts."

David speaks about worship with such joy! He talks about crying aloud or *rejoicing* — a word that implies whirling around in an exalted dance before the Lord! No, sir, this Psalm is definitely *not* a downer! It is the most victorious kind of experience!

None of us lives without failure — the kind of failure that displeases God or attacks the authority of His purpose in our lives. Sin isn't just unrighteousness or transgression of the Law or doing evil. It also includes not doing the good you know to do. Sin is acting out of fear instead of faith. Sin is falling short of God's ultimate purpose in our lives. *All of these are sin.*

Some folks are more predictably weak than others. People born in righteous, godly circumstances and raised in the Word of God have a great advantage over those born in negative, ungodly environments. As those in the latter category grow up, difficult circumstances literally fill their lives with dangerous potentials that never occur to the person born into a godly environment.

But may we never forget that there is power through the blood of Jesus Christ! We also have the power of the Holy Spirit at our disposal to live victoriously over any temptation or sin. That's the bottom line! However, *when we do fail and miss the mark* — when we don't complete God's purposes for us — there is a redemptive process and a God of covenant love and maternal tenderness who wants not only to forgive but to redeem even the circumstances of our failure.

The question is not whether or not you failed. The question is, how will you respond when you *do* fail?

When David saw his restoration by faith, he saw it full and complete. That total healing would enable ministry and teaching to flow out of his life in a pure and undefiled manner. *God was exalted by that process.* David became a happy, fulfilled, and exuberant worshiper, released once more into the Presence and the purposes of God.

This book can't produce repentance or change people's spirits. Nevertheless, no one has read these words by coincidence. Wherever there is a need for change, renewal, and the humble honesty that leads toward repentance, *the Holy Spirit will stop Heaven to move on the behalf of anyone whose spirit is open.*

As you read these words, you may have sensed your own need for personal renewal. Ask God to put the price on repentance and renewal for your life. What would repentance mean for you? How would it happen? What would renewal look like? Ask the Lord to be specific. He *will* answer — He cares that much for you!

When you have your answer, you can then pray from your heart:

Father, I ask You to complete what You are doing in my life. Lord, I want to deal with the vital need for restoration in my heart. I cry to You for renewal! I ask You, Lord, to confirm and complete whatever work needs to be done in my life. In Jesus' Name. Amen.

PSALM 102

Fifth of the Penitential Psalms

So the Psalm, which begins with the humble prayer of the penitent that God will not hide His face from him in the time of trouble, ends with the act of faith of the pardoned soul that He should dwell in God's unveiled Presence throughout eternity in that kingdom where no trouble can ever come.[1]

— Alfred G. Mortimer
Notes on the Seven Penitential Psalms

CHAPTER 5

Discipline and Restoration

Psalm 102

℗SALM *102*

Hear my prayer, O Lord, and let my cry come to You.

Do not hide Your face from me in the day of my trouble; incline Your ear to me; in the day that I call, answer me speedily.

For my days are consumed like smoke, and my bones are burned like a hearth.

My heart is stricken and withered like grass, so that I forget to eat my bread.

Because of the sound of my groaning my bones cling to my skin.

I am like a pelican of the wilderness; I am like an owl of the desert.

I lie awake, and am like a sparrow alone on the housetop.

My enemies reproach me all day long, those who deride me swear an oath against me.

For I have eaten ashes like bread, and mingled my drink with weeping,

Because of Your indignation and Your wrath; for You have lifted me up and cast me away.

My days are like a shadow that lengthens, and I wither away like grass.

But You, O Lord, shall endure forever, and the remembrance of Your name to all generations.

You will arise and have mercy on Zion; for the time to favor her, yes, the set time, has come.

For Your servants take pleasure in her stones, and show favor to her dust.

So the nations shall fear the name of the LORD, and all the kings of the earth Your glory.

For the Lord shall build up Zion; he shall appear in His glory.

He shall regard the prayer of the destitute, and shall not despise their prayer.

This will be written for the generation to come, that a people yet to be created may praise the Lord.

For He looked down from the height of His sanctuary; from heaven the Lord viewed the earth,

To hear the groaning of the prisoner, to release those appointed to death,

To declare the name of the Lord in Zion, and His praise in Jerusalem,

When the peoples are gathered together, and the kingdoms, to serve the Lord.

He weakened my strength in the way; he shortened my days.

I said, "O my God, do not take me away in the midst of my days; your years are throughout all generations.

Of old You laid the foundation of the earth, and the heavens are the work of Your hands.

They will perish, but You will endure; yes, they will all grow old like a garment; like a cloak You will change them, and they will be changed.

But You are the same, and Your years will have no end.

The children of Your servants will continue, and their descendants will be established before You."

*D*o you remember from your school days the traditional seven wonders of the ancient world? I wonder how many of them you could still identify — the pyramids of Egypt, the hanging gardens of Babylon, the lighthouse of Alexandria, and so on.

Recently *The Sunday Times Magazine* of London asked several well-known persons to choose the seven wonders of the modern world. Needless to say, this resulted in a lot of debate. Lord Kenneth Clark selected the Concord aircraft as one of his seven wonders. A famous photographer included American hamburgers on his list, and novelist Anthony Burgess said champagne was high on his list of the seven wonders of the modern world. Another novelist mentioned Disneyland, while others selected New York City, the great wall of China, the city of Venice, and the Taj Mahal.

It is very clear that in both the ancient and the modern lists, something important is left out. *The human being* is truly a wonder of the world!

We Are God's Workmanship

In truth, we are the masterpiece of God's creation and the wonder of wonders because God came to earth and became one of us. He did this to tell us how much He loved us and to bring us into the fulfillment of His purpose. No greater wonder exists than this divine expression of love!

Ephesians 2:10 reads, "For we are His workmanship, created in Christ Jesus for good works, which God prepared beforehand that we should walk in them." The word "workmanship" in the Greek is *poiema*, from which we get our English word "poem." This particular word is only used twice in the New Testament. In Romans 1:20, it is used in reference to the natural creation of the earth as a grand revelation of God's purpose. But in Ephesians 2:10, it is *man himself* who is the poem, or the creative workmanship, of God.

It is important to remember that you are God's workmanship when you sense the divine "nudge" toward repentance. You see, God isn't mad at you. He is not trying to box you into some kind of negative, life-defeating lifestyle. Repentance is as positive as the body's natural mechanisms to throw off poison or to exhale stagnant, lifeless air.

True repentance is accompanied by God's overwhelming grace. Our entire existence should be a lifestyle of repentance and grace. Repentance and grace go together like love and marriage, like breathing out and breathing in.

God's purpose for each of us is dynamic, freeing, fruitful and joy-filled. But, of course, He will not force us to pursue that purpose. God offers us His supreme treasure, but He wants us to come to Him freely and to respond to His grace.

We can live as far away from God's purpose as we desire to, and He won't stop loving us. There's not a thing in this world we can do to cause God to cease from loving us. But although we don't have to respond to His purpose, it is clear what He wants us to be: His workmanship made clear and untarnished.

John Newton, who wrote the song "Amazing Grace," had lived for years in a most debauched way as a slave trader. He wrote the song as a result of his experience with Christ. Following his conversion, he became a minister at a small country church, where he spent much of his ministry. In the end, he was called from that small country church to a very large church in the great city of London, England.

When he received his summons, John offered a fervent prayer for what he called "London grace." Asked what he meant by "London grace," John replied with a twinkle in his eye, "London grace is a grace of a high degree. It is a very intense grace; it is a very special grace; it is a grace strong enough to make it possible for me to live the Christian life, even in London."

Newton's prayer is appropriate whether we live in San Francisco, New York City, Des Moines, Montreal, Paris, Casa Blanca, or Beirut. Wherever we live, God's amazing grace, combined with our response of repentance, makes it possible for us to live a life in the spirit of His divine love.

A Look at the Territory of Psalm 102

The fifth of the Penitential Psalms is Psalm 102. Although many sections of this Psalm appear to be an individual's lament or complaint, the preponderance of the Psalm is of a corporate nature. Where the psalmist speaks about Zion, we can also say "the Church" or "the Body of Christ." In the long run, Psalm 102 is a statement about God's ultimate desire and purpose for His people, whether Israel under the Old Covenant or His Church of individual believers under the New Covenant.

I confess to you that as I studied the seven Penitential Psalms, this was the one I dreaded the most. I thought it was such a negative Psalm. But all that changed quickly as I began to study Psalm 102. I now recognize that it is filled with truths that speak to my spirit. I pray I can adequately share these significant, life-changing truths with you.

This is a highly complex Psalm. Leslie Allen, a professor at Fuller Theological Seminary, writes the following in one of the newest commentaries: "A bewildering multiplicity of interpretations have been offered for this complex psalm."[2] When you isolate portions of it, it seems like an individual is crying to the Lord. Yet other portions of the Psalm are obviously corporate, speaking about God's people in general. Leslie Allen writes further, "This psalm bears an abundance of evidence of skillful technical construction as a vehicle for its thought."[3]

One of the obvious complexities is that although Psalm 102 is a Penitential Psalm, not a single mention of sin is made in the entire Psalm. Consequently, there is no confession of sin. Since the very concept of the seven Penitential Psalms is repentance or confession of sin, it leaves us with a question similar to the one we asked regarding Psalm 6. Why is Psalm 102 a Penitential Psalm?

The answer may be found in an issue that we all can relate to — the times in our lives when we must pay for other people's mistakes or problems. Now, that's common territory for all of us, isn't it?

Perhaps, for example, this Psalm may have something to do with the 70-year Babylonian captivity of God's people. The writer says he has suffered "because of Your indignation and Your wrath; for You have lifted me up and cast me away. My days are like a shadow that lengthens, and I wither away like grass" (Psalm 102:10,11). The psalmist's words could be paraphrased: "I was taken out of my country and put far away in another country because of Your indignation against my people — not because of any specific sin in my own life." Does that help you identify with the situation?

Many scholars suggest that either Ezra or Nehemiah wrote Psalm 102. It may very well have come out of that time period of captivity and ultimate restoration. Others say that Daniel wrote this Psalm, since it appears to be written by a captive who is still in Babylon and still paying the price for the sins of his fathers. The words of the Psalm suggest that the separation and judgment of God are still upon His people. The writer's hope, then, is for a restoration not yet begun.

I might add that another theory points to David as the author of Psalm 102. If that is true, his words were a prophetic foretelling of future events that were yet to come.

At any rate, Psalm 102 was written by a person who deeply identified with the corporate people of God and whose suffering was related to God's judgment on His people. The psalmist is also a man with great faith and expectation that God's people will ultimately be restored.

You see, identifying with God's people is a broader issue than just jumping in when revival is raging. The Church has too many "fair-weather sailors" who choose on a day-to-day basis what group they belong to.

When the judgment of society and, sometimes, the judgment of God come upon the corporate Church in a nation, it is no longer culturally popular or even acceptable to be a Christian. We have seen this happen in China, Russia and many other countries. These are the moments when an instant division often occurs between serious believers and those who are only looking out for their own best interests.

Some people accept only a casual identity with the Church or with the Israel of God. These people think they are free to join the cynics who criticize and tell ribald jokes at the expense of Christians. With the recent, very public exposure of high-placed Christians, most believers in this country have been tested on this issue. It is so easy to join the crowd and snicker with the rest!

But that is certainly not the case of the psalmist in Psalm 102. This psalmist understands, as we have already discussed in a previous study, that the call for repentance is *an imperatively corporate process*.

In Hebrews 1, the Father God quotes Psalm 102:25-27 concerning His Son, Jesus. This is, in fact, the longest section of a Psalm quoted in the New Testament.

> **Of old You laid the foundation of the earth, and the heavens are the work of Your hands.**
>
> **They will perish, but You will endure; yes, they will all grow old like a garment; like a cloak You will change them, and they will be changed.**
>
> **But You are the same, and Your years will have no end.**
>
> **Psalm 102:25-27**

Because this passage is quoted in Hebrews 1 in reference to Jesus, many Bible teachers (such as Gaebelein, for whose writings I have a deep and abiding respect) think that this entire Psalm must apply to the Messiah. They believe the Psalm is referring to the sufferings of the entire Church descending upon Jesus — judgment for sins He did not commit. These Bible teachers also believe that verses 10 and 11 refer to Jesus when He was cast away from the Presence of the Father as the Sin-Bearer.

The Organization of Psalm 102

The organizational structure of Psalm 102 shows three main stanzas. As in some of the other Penitential

Psalms, the first stanza of this Psalm is a lament and includes the first 11 verses. The key words of this first section are probably "my days" or "my day."

Each of us do have a very limited period of time in this world. That period of time is "our day," and we are the ones who choose what to do with it.

During a one-year sabbatical as I read through the Bible, I wrote specific dates in the margins next to scriptures the Lord quickened to my heart. In Johannesburg, South Africa, on April the third, at the very end of that one year, God underlined in my spirit Psalm 92:10: "But my horn You have exalted like a wild ox; I have been anointed with fresh oil." In the margin I wrote, "O God, for that to happen!"

The words in Psalm 92:14 are also underlined: "They shall still bear fruit in old age; they shall be fresh and flourishing." Again written in the margin of my Bible are the words, "O God!"

Get it straight. Your days are either spent in the accumulation of "doing your own thing," or they become part of a greater picture. That's the choice this psalmist faced in Psalm 102. He could focus on his own suffering and circumstantial difficulties, or he could somehow see a broader perspective that encompassed the corporate body of God's people.

This difference in spiritual perspective is similar to the situation of four men who were working together on a great building. Someone asked one of them, "What are you doing?"

The man answered, "I'm laying concrete."

Then one of the other men was asked, "What are you doing?"

"I'm putting up studs," he reported.

The same question was addressed to the third man: "What are *you* doing?"

"I'm working on doors," the third man commented.

Finally, the fourth man was asked, "What are you doing?"

He answered with a smile, "I'm building a cathedral!"

It's all in the perspective, isn't it? Some lay concrete, put up studs, birth children, build houses, go to jobs, earn money, pay taxes, die and are buried. *Other people submit their years and days to a divine purpose that is much broader and far beyond the pursuit of their simple survival.*

The second section of Psalm 102 includes verses 12-22. This passage is a statement of incredible confidence in the ultimate purpose of God. The prominent word in this section is the mention of the divine name *Yahweh*. This name is used seven times in this Psalm! Scholars often categorize specific Psalms as "Elohimic" because, as in Psalm 51 (David's last Penitential Psalm), the psalmist uses the name *Elohim* for God. *Elohim* is actually the most prominent word for God in the Hebrew culture.

But *Yahweh*, the unspoken name for God that is often translated "Jehovah" or "Lord" is *only* used in Psalm 102. The psalmist doesn't use *Adonai* or *Elohim* once — only *Yahweh*!

Yahweh is formed from three verb tenses, carrying the meaning of "the God who was and who is and who shall be." Yahweh is the God who causes something to come into existence out of nothing!

Finally, the last section of Psalm 102 is the passage that later becomes a primary New Testament quote in the book of Hebrews. This stanza makes a clear contrast between human weakness and the eternalness of God.

Let's Apply This Psalm

I once heard a story about a married couple who visited a shopping mall and stopped at a wishing well in the center of the arcade. The wife playfully tossed in a coin, but the husband just stood there for a while, wistfully looking into the water. Finally, he threw his coin in. "What did you wish for?" the wife asked.

The husband answered, "I just wished I could afford whatever it is *you* wished for!"

That's actually an important understanding that can be applied to all our lives. It is one thing to want a dynamic life filled with breathing in the very atmosphere of God's Presence. It's wonderful to want our years to count as a vital expression of God's purpose. But it is altogether a different thing to be willing to pay the price — to know and accept what it really costs to link up with divine purpose.

The Connection Between Repentance and Intercession

Practically applied, Psalm 102 teaches us about the intercessory nature of true repentance. In true intercessory prayer, the person praying must identify with those for whom he is praying. This identity factor of intercessory prayer must also accompany true repentance and is an outstanding aspect of Psalm 102.

In the personal lament (verses 1-11), no mention is made of actual sin. However, it is in this section that the writer says God's indignation and wrath have cast him away (verse 10). The Hebrew word translated "cast" carries the meaning of being caught up in a whirlwind, swept away from one's homeland and carried to a far-off land of exiles.

Thus, the writer is broken through this history and becomes a byword to the heathen. This is basic to the understanding of Psalm 102. As the psalmist describes not only his own pain, but the pain of his exiled people, he reveals the identity factor that is part of true intercession.

Hear my prayer, O Lord, and let my cry come to You.

Do not hide Your face from me in the day of my trouble; incline Your ear to me; in the day that I call, answer me speedily.

For my days are consumed like smoke, and my bones are burned like a hearth.

My heart is stricken and withered like grass, so that I forget to eat my bread.

Because of the sound of my groaning my bones cling to my skin.

I am like a pelican of the wilderness; I am like an owl of the desert.

I lie awake, and am like a sparrow alone on the housetop.

My enemies reproach me all day long, those who deride me swear an oath against me.

For I have eaten ashes like bread, and mingled my drink with weeping,

Because of Your indignation and Your wrath; for You have lifted me up and cast me away.

My days are like a shadow that lengthens, and I wither away like grass.

Psalm 102:1-11

These are very difficult words, aren't they? This is an almost *inexplicable* lament, written by an individual caught in the whirlwind of corporate judgment.

Why should we study this Psalm? The answer is obvious. Almost all of us at one time or another must live out the results of *other* people's decisions. We must also walk through times of national or church bewilderment.

Please stay with this a moment. There are three parallel passages in the Bible that are master studies on intercession. These passages of Scripture are Daniel 9, Ezra 9, and Nehemiah 9. In each of these accounts, we find three great men caught up and cast away — not because of their personal sin, but as a result of God's judgment and its ultimate consequences upon their nation.

Although caught in these storms of history, each of these men of God became successful in their own lives as they allowed God to use and bless their talents to His glory. Thus, these three men became extremely important to the culture in which they lived. None of them forgot where their hearts lay, for each man constantly turned toward Jerusalem.

I urge you to personally study the prayers of Daniel, Ezra, and Nehemiah, located in the ninth chapters of the books bearing their names. Each prayer shouts to the issues of Psalm 102.

The psalmist ultimately says, "You will arise and have mercy on Zion; for the time to favor her, yes, the set time, has come" (Psalm 102:13). This is reminiscent of Daniel's revelation as he read Jeremiah's judgment prophecy. Daniel realized that the designated time of judgment was 70 years, and that that 70 years had just been completed!

Daniel had been one of the first to go into captivity. *How well he could count those seventy years!* Why wasn't Daniel bitter? Why hadn't he moaned all those years, "Why me? What have I done to deserve this punishment?" To make Daniel's situation even more difficult, Jerusalem was still intact during the first half of his captivity! Most of the people in Israel were still living there in their sin and complacency. But Daniel was trapped in a foreign land, far away from family and his people.

How easily Daniel could have said, "How unfair of God to do this!" *Instead, he surrendered his life to the purposes of God. Out of that surrender arose a man of excellent character to whom God could reveal more of the future than to any other person in the Old Testament.*

Daniel's intercessional identity is very evident in the following verses. He writes:

> In the first year of Darius the son of Ahasuerus, of the lineage of the Medes, who was made king over the realm of the Chaldeans.
>
> In the first year of his reign I, Daniel, understood by the books the number of the years specified by the word of the Lord through Jeremiah the prophet, that He would accomplish seventy years in the desolations of Jerusalem [referring to Jeremiah 25:11 and 2 Chronicles 6:21].
>
> Then I set my face toward the Lord God to make request by prayer and supplications, with fasting, sackcloth and ashes.
>
> Daniel 9:1-3

But what about you? Do you plan on living your life for you, your wife, your son John and his wife — you four and no more? If you do, I have news for you. You have a totally limited perspective and a very narrow playing field on which to live out your mundane existence. God wants to lift you up beyond that to a higher level of living!

The place in which a believer finds himself in his spiritual walk is never an accident. It all depends on how he responds when a little suffering comes and the squeeze begins. It's so easy to try to get out from under the pain. If the pressure pertains to a specific church, the person may look in the Saturday newspaper to find another church to attend the next morning. Instead of responding to God's dealings, he may decide to go with the easy solution: "Let's find another place."

Thank God, there are people with a different kind of character! These people say, "God has placed us here. We identify with God's purposes even when those purposes are difficult."

Local churches in this country were often built in the most difficult historical moments in American history. The people who built these churches had the attitude, "Ease has nothing to do with it. The question is, what does *God* want us to do?" Then they went on to fulfill the purposes of God. *They understood the identity factor of repentance and restoration.*

Our Future Is as Bright as the Character of God

The hope in all repentance must ultimately be based on the character of God. The hope for change isn't based on a promise that we will never fail again. Nor is it based on reading the Bible or even praying more, as good as these practices are. The hope for change and renewal through repentance is fundamentally based upon the character of God.

We have already seen that this Psalm is unique in its use of the name *Yahweh* seven different times (eight times, if you include the superscription over the Psalm). In Exodus 3:15, God says,

> Moreover God said to Moses, "Thus you shall say to the children of Israel: 'The Lord God of your fathers, the God of Abraham, the God of Isaac, and the God of Jacob, has sent me to you. This is My name forever, and this is My memorial to all generations.'"

Remember, Yahweh is a combination of three Hebrew verbs meaning "was" (past existence); "am" (present existence); and "I shall be" (future existence).

Therefore, this name of God speaks of the three basic tenses of life and involvement.

An acquaintance and scholar, Dr. John Ogilvie, who is currently Chaplain of the United States Senate, writes, "There is something else in that name Yahweh, because it really means the God or the One who causes things to exist."[4] God is not only self-existent, but He brings into existence that which is not. He is a creative reality. He can make something of nothing. His very name speaks of our hope.

Jehovah is committed to covenant. Several times in Psalm 102, the name "Zion" is used in reference to God's promises of mercy — of a set time and a specific work that He will yet do.

God keeps his commitments! Friends may sometimes fail friends. Spouses may even decide, based on certain involvements, not to spend their lives with their mates. We have all witnessed the separation of friendships and families in these types of situations. Covenants in our culture are not often seen as "forever" commitments.

But when the same God who has made a covenant with you says something is true, it is *always* going to be true! Even if He must judge and deal with you for a season, He doesn't cast you away forever. He has a covenant with you.

Where have you placed your confidence? What are you building your hope on? Is it Wall Street, the "American Dream," your currency standards? Oh, surely not, my friend!

Cultures around the world have been forced to devalue their currencies. You see, the standard for our world is *change*. There is no security in any manmade system.

Is your faith in a governmental structure? I read a funny story in *The Boston Globe* many years ago. It was shortly after the election of John Kennedy to the presidency. The President was chatting with a conservative industrialist about the economy. Kennedy remarked offhandedly, "If I weren't President, I'd be buying stocks right now."

The businessman replied with a smile, "Yes, and if you weren't President, *I'd* be buying stocks right now."

Where have you placed *your* confidence? God keeps His covenant. That's an unfailing hope you can count on!

God also possesses an unchanging faithfulness to His Word. That's why we must pray *His Word*, not our feelings or emotions! Our hope of repentance isn't "God, I'll be a better boy. I'll do a better job." The hope of repentance must be "God, *this is Your Word.*"

Look intensely at what the psalmist says in verse 13: "You will arise and have mercy on Zion; For the time to favor her, *Yes, the set time, has come*" (Psalm 102:13). The psalmist isn't reciting a shopping list of things he wants from God. He is just reminding God of His own promises.

So start praying what God has said. That's the guarantee that it will happen!

But in addition to God's name, His covenant, and His Word is the *unfailing issue of His compassion.* The psalmist writes:

> This will be written for the generation to come, that a people yet to be created may praise the Lord.
>
> For He looked down from the height of His sanctuary; *from heaven the Lord viewed the earth,*
>
> *To hear the groaning of the prisoner, to release those appointed to death,*

To declare the name of the Lord in Zion, and His praise in Jerusalem.

Psalm 102:18-21

As you read this passage, don't you immediately think of the words of Isaiah?

The Spirit of the Lord God is upon Me, because the Lord has anointed Me to preach good tidings to the poor; he has sent Me to heal the brokenhearted, to proclaim liberty to the captives and the opening of the prison to those who are bound;

To proclaim the acceptable year of the Lord....

Isaiah 61:1,2

God *wants* to liberate the captives. He wants to set prisoners free because that's who He is! He is a God of compassion.

God's Faithfulness Is Eternal

The Psalm also speaks of God's externality in verses 25-27, which we have already quoted. God will forever be there for us! People won't.

The New Testament application of this passage is very important. Hebrews 1 is a great chapter for people who are facing pressure and tribulation or for those who are being tempted to give up their faith in Jesus Christ. It seemed so much simpler for these Hebrew Christians to go back to the more secure and politically approved system of religiosity and ritual.

But the writer to the Hebrews warns, "Don't ever do that. The prophets, the Aaronic priesthood, and the ritualistic system under the Old Covenant are all passing. There is only One who is eternal — the One of whom Jehovah said, 'You remain the same *[referring to Jesus Christ]*, and Your years will not fail'" (Hebrews 1:12).

Do you enjoy looking at mountains? I do. I can sit for a long time contemplating beautiful mountains. The physical place where I have spent most of my ministry is varied and beautiful, with ocean, mountains, and valleys. I have never been able to complain about the challenges of that specific state.

I believe there is a wrong spirit in many believers' lives that makes them complain about the regions in which they live. I thank God every week for San Francisco, for the Bay Area and for Redwood City. When I hear Christians talk negatively about the place God has put them, I know the enemy is at work in that area of their lives. He is creating discontentment and ultimately making them spiritually ineffective in their own homes and communities.

When I fly to my home from one of the many places in our world where I minister, the beauty of the mountains and the proximity of the ocean always overwhelms me. I never get tired of standing in my city and taking in the phenomena of the beautiful land that surrounds me. It's wonderful! But one day, it will all be rolled up like a scroll and will vanish. Only God remains eternal.

Never Lose Sight of the Big Picture

Our love of Zion, or of God's corporate people, and our concern for His corporate purpose is foundational to our relationship with God. It's truly the foundation of grace and repentance.

You will arise and have mercy on Zion; for the time to favor her, yes, the set time, has come.

For Your servants take pleasure in her stones, and show favor to her dust.

Psalm 102:13,14

Have you ever been around Christians who speak disparagingly about the Church or the corporate nature of God's purposes? I confess to you that I have. Unfortunately, I have also taken part in that kind of conversation.

It is so easy to join the ribald discussions of the world about the corporate nature of the Church. For instance, Christians sometimes say, "I want to go to Heaven, but I can't stand the thought of living with Christians for eternity." How many times have you heard that?

When believers participate in that kind of conversation, they allow a subtle working of an ungodly principle into their lives. God favors people who love His *corporate* purpose.

Consider Daniel, who spent 70 years as a hostage in captivity for no fault of his own. Although Daniel's prison was a palace, he could never whitewash out of his spirit God's corporate purpose for his people.

For some of us, it takes only one or two little disappointments with other Christians to make us discard our identity with God's corporate purpose and retreat to our own agendas and personal activities. This response won't cause us to miss eternity. I'm sure we'll still get to Heaven; however, we'll arrive there lonely, isolated, and fruitless. Ah, friend! Only by participating in God's corporate purpose will we find productivity and purpose.

Over the years, I have witnessed elements of judgment fall publicly on several major Christian ministries. In some instances, these ministries operated out of what I believe was a judgmental and condemning spirit. Yet I have also watched with horror as the majority of believers reacted in judgment rather than in compassion to these ministries' problems.

We must all constantly endeavor to keep the overall, corporate purposes of God in perspective. That's why it is so important to pray *with the intercession of identity* for the true restoration and redemption of every difficult circumstance.

The Ultimate Purpose For Renewal

The ultimate purpose for the kind of renewal the psalmist prays for in Psalm 102 is *missions*: "So the nations shall fear the name of the Lord, and all the kings of the earth Your glory" (Psalm 102:15). We see here that this writer is not only involving himself with God's greater purpose, but also with God's ultimate restoration or renewal. *God's purpose is life.* He is the Lord of the infinite dynamic.

The writer adds, "This will be written for the generation to come, that a people yet to be created may praise the Lord" (Psalm 102:18). Do we genuinely have a concern for the people of the future?

When I was growing up, I frequently heard from adults, "We're not doing this or that because we want to leave an inheritance for our children." These parents lived simply to put aside for their children. On the other hand, today we often hear parents say almost sarcastically, "We're spending our children's inheritance!"

Now, I clearly believe that believers have a stewardship responsibility regarding what they leave behind after their death. For instance, it would be tragic to leave large amounts of money to children who do not serve God. However, I believe Christians have a much more important responsibility to say, "I know there is a divine purpose for the future. I commit myself and lay my life down as a bridge toward that future purpose."

We have heard from Daniel as he prayed in the midst of his own captivity in Babylon. Now this psalmist confesses not only a future but a divine purpose for a people not yet born! I am told that this section of Psalm 102 in the original Hebrew suggests a *resurrection* — a new generation that blooms like spring flowers out of what seemed to be infinite death.

Who can forget the similar experience of the prophet Ezekiel? God took him to a great valley that was filled with dry bones, disconnected and bleached in the desert sand. God asked, "…Son of man, can these bones live?…"(Ezekiel 37:3).

Ezekiel responds in an almost hopeless faith, "…O Lord God, You know."

God's answer to Ezekiel has been a *foundational principle* for my ministry:

> …Prophesy to these bones, and say to them, 'O dry bones, hear the word of the Lord!
>
> 'Thus says the Lord God to these bones: "Surely I will cause breath to enter into you, and you shall live."'
>
> **Ezekiel 37:4,5**

Believe me, I'm often reminded of this valley of dry bones during some of my Sunday morning services! So what good is preaching? Well, the proclamation of truth is God's primary method for bringing resurrection. That's why it is so important not to sit through a sermon thinking, *Come on, get it over with!*

Do you believe that life will come forth to you through the sermon you are hearing? I do! I believe the agency God has created for renewal is His Word. I think He has created the foolishness of preaching to save those who will believe. When the preacher proclaims or prophesies the Word, the Holy Spirit enters into "dead bones" and life comes as God breathes forth resurrection power!

The Promise of the Generations To Come

So this psalmist believes in a future yet *unborn* in the midst of the present lifeless circumstances that surround him. Again I stress, reader, that the best guarantee *you* can have for the future is to identify with God's purposes.

The Psalm ends by saying, "The children of Your servants will continue, and their descendants will be established before You" (verse 28). What phenomenal foresight. What a victorious understanding!

A very similar scripture is found in Psalm 78:6,7: "That the generation to come might know them, the children who would be born, that they may arise and declare them to their children, That they may set their hope in God, and not forget the works of God, but keep His commandments." Next to this passage in my Bible is a note I wrote in the margin: "For Jeff and Cheri, 9-21-86."

Cheri is my daughter, and Jeff is her husband. They now have four sons and a daughter. Those children and grandchildren are the manifestation of God's promise to us!

It is more than just a matter of progenity, or of having children and grandchildren. Sure, in the natural, there is something wonderful even about that. But how much greater is the blessing of seeing the next generations come to know and stand by faith on the same divine promises and covenant you have embraced! *That* is true life!

When others are birthed into God's Kingdom out of your concern and identity with His people, that is *spiritual* progenity. God's promise is that this new generation and their children will have a covenant with Him.

Personally, I would rather that my children and grandchildren, both natural and spiritual, possess the heritage of my faith in God's Word and of His corporate promise to the Church than that they have bank accounts or trust funds to see them through financially.

You can see how this Psalm is incredibly personal. Our lives must also be lived out in similar situations. We often can't control the circumstances of our lives, but we *can* control our attitude, our faith and our hope!

I earnestly desire that you receive from the spirit of this psalmist. Then you, too, can obtain hope through personal restoration, repentance, and God's grace as you identify with the corporate purposes of God.

It pays to be concerned about the Body of Christ as this psalmist was for Israel — to be broken-hearted over sin and to confess in true repentance. That's the way you begin to understand and identify with God's heart-cry regarding His people and His purpose. You begin to claim the promises God has given concerning the Church and what He purposes to do in the last days. You also learn to share His heart for renewal and set that goal as the aspiration of your own heart.

As you begin to identify with God's broader, corporate purpose, suddenly something happens. You yourself are lifted closer and closer to the throne of God!

This psalmist prays for personal renewal and freshness, yet he doesn't forget his identity with his entire people. From a description of his own loneliness, depression, physical problems and persecution suffered at the hands of his enemies, he moves quickly to a recognition of God's corporate purpose, identifying with what God has said concerning His people.

Once the psalmist's heart begins to identify with his people, he finds new purpose himself. He begins to see God in His eternalness. He realizes that God has things under control. Suddenly peace begins to reign. He can end the Psalm speaking not only about his own life being restored, but of generations of children living in the purposes of God. What a miracle that a psalmist who started in such personal distress could end with that kind of faith!

Have you set your heart upon God's purposes in Zion — on the corporate body of the Church world-wide? Are you right now walking through a time of sorrow and a deep sense of repentance for the many ways the Church has corporately missed God's purpose? If so, let deep faith spring up in you for what God will yet do through His people!

Perhaps at the end of this quick study of Psalm 102, you also realize a need for personal repentance. Have you surrendered to the circumstances of the present and thus lost your faith for the future? Do you need a new grace for repentance in your personal life? Let me also close this chapter with a personal prayer you can adopt as your own:

Lord, You are bringing to many of Your children both a corporate and personal identification with repentance and Your grace. I ask that You graciously work that work in *my* heart and life. In Jesus' Name. Amen.

PSALM 130

Sixth of the Penitential Psalms

At a certain occasion Martin Luther was asked what were the best Psalms. He answered by saying "Psalmi Paulini," the Pauline Psalms. When they wanted to know what the Pauline Psalms are he replied, "The thirty-second, the fifty-first, the one hundred and thirtieth and the one hundred and forty-third." He explained that these Psalms teach us that the forgiveness of sins is vouchsafed to all who believe without having any works of the law to offer. They are therefore Pauline Psalms.

The entire race is in the depths of sin and death, and the only way out is to cry unto Jehovah; as man cannot save himself, Jehovah must save him.[1]

— Arno C. Gaebelein

CHAPTER 6

Forgiveness, Patience, and Assurance
Psalm 130

*P*SALM *130*

Out of the depths I have cried to You, O Lord;

Lord, hear my voice! Let Your ears be attentive to the voice of my supplications.

If You, Lord, should mark iniquities, O Lord, who could stand?

But there is forgiveness with You, that You may be feared.

I wait for the Lord, my soul waits, and in His word I do hope.

My soul waits for the Lord more than those who watch for the morning — yes, more than those who watch for the morning.

O Israel, hope in the Lord; for with the Lord there is mercy, and with Him is abundant redemption.

And He shall redeem Israel from all his iniquities.

*F*rances Bacon reportedly said, "It is not what we eat, but what we *digest* that makes us strong. It is not what we gain, but what we *save* that makes us rich. It is not what we read, but what we *remember* that makes us learned. *And it is not what we preach, but what we practice that makes us Christian.*"

How many times in childhood were you told, "Practice makes perfect"? I firmly believe that whether or not you possess inner peace — the peace that results from a committed Christian life — depends on your willingness to practice that which God has said to you. In order to live in continual peace, you must lay aside the monotonous and mundane things of life that so often choke out life within your experience.

There is an amusing little cartoon strip in which a tiny insect is looking up at a much larger specimen in the insect world. Expressing all the puzzlement the cartoonist could put in the little bug's face, the tiny insect asks, "What kind of insect are you?"

"I'm a praying mantis," comes the answer from the larger insect.

The little one replies, "That's absurd — insects don't pray."

Whereupon the praying mantis grabs the tiny bug by the throat and begins to squeeze. Caught in this desperate situation, his bulging eyes rolling heavenward, the tiny bug begins to pray, "Our Father who art in heaven..."

The cartoon, of course, is pointing to an inescapable truth we have all dealt with: *pain and suffering are among life's most powerful motivating forces*. That's one of the difficult lessons we have to learn about the human condition and particularly about our own religious experience.

As Christians, we affirm and proclaim the resurrection power of Jesus Christ. Our calling is to follow Jesus into certain well-defined and fulfilling ways of life. We are to commit ourselves to a lifestyle in which Jesus' teaching is reflected in our personal lives. We know this. We hear this message preached regularly from the pulpit. We come to church; we pray about it; we sing about it; we think about it; and we praise God for promising abundant life to us.

Yet true fulfillment is not something to which we readily commit. Too often we remain unmoved and unmotivated. Instead of genuinely committing to the rule of Christ in our lives, we put God on hold. We pray, "Show us Your abundant life, O Lord — but not now."

Then disaster strikes and panic comes. Out of the depths of our pain and suffering, we cry out like that little insect, "Our Father who art in heaven!" Yet even in that condition, Jesus will answer us if our prayer is sincere and our hearts are genuinely open to His response — *whatever* it may be. The Lord will stand before us and say, "Why are you troubled? Why are you questioning? Rise up in your heart! See My hands; see My feet, that it is I Myself. Handle me; touch Me."

We recognize Christ's Presence by willingly acknowledging His resurrection power at work in our situation to change both us and our circumstances. In doing so, we discover the supreme sign that God is always with us: Jesus is here. He is with us now in our midst, in good times and in bad. This is something we all need to know.

From Despair to Resurrection!

The sixth of the Penitential Psalms is the 130th Psalm. As mentioned earlier, Christians have separated these seven unique Psalms from the rest since the second century — long before denominations existed. The church has used them as a miniature Psalter to identify with the temptations of Jesus during the season called "Christian Lent."

Psalm 130 is much like the opening story of the tiny insect because it begins with the words, "Out of the depths." In fact, a major musical work written from this Psalm is centered around that very first word of the Latin text — *de profundis*, which means "out of the depths." We might actually translate this word "from the despairs."

But hold on! You may be surprised that Psalm 130 makes a moving transition. It may begin in the depths, but it doesn't stay there. It moves from *depths* to *answers*, and that is where we find hope! By the end of this Psalm, there is a resurrection.

Psalm 130 is not only the sixth of the Penitential Psalms, but it is also the eleventh step in the 15 Psalms of *ascent*, or of *degrees*. It speaks not only about repentance, but about entering into *true* worship. The end is coming to know God in reality!

This is a short Psalm with only eight verses. Read these verses carefully, for that is more important than anything anyone could say about them.

Out of the depths I have cried to You, O Lord;

Lord, hear my voice! Let Your ears be attentive to the voice of my supplications.

If You, Lord, should mark iniquities, O Lord, who could stand?

But there is forgiveness with You, that You may be feared.

I wait for the Lord, my soul waits, and in His word I do hope.

My soul waits for the Lord more than those who watch for the morning — yes, more than those who watch for the morning.

O Israel, hope in the Lord; for with the Lord there is mercy, and with Him is abundant redemption.

And He shall redeem Israel from all his iniquities.

Psalm 130:1-8

What a way to begin a Psalm of praise! "Out of the depths!" Yet who among us could not identify with this condition? We face so many different kinds of "out of the depths" experiences as we go through life.

Someone else's words can hit you like a dash of cold water in your face or like a blow that sends you reeling into the depths. Perhaps someone has said to you, "I'm sorry; I just don't love you anymore." Or maybe someone in authority at your workplace told you, "You've done a great job. However, we're going to have to do some streamlining around this place, and your position is being eliminated."

Your "out of the depths" experience may have come to you in a doctor's office when someone said, "We have the results from the lab, and I'm afraid it's cancer." Perhaps you were standing in the hospital hallway when you heard the words, "Your wife is fine, but the baby didn't make it."

You see, these are the kinds of situations this Psalm is about. Words that come to mind are *stillborn, death, funeral* and *disappointment in relationships*. One person has written, "The 130th Psalm is written for the *heavy* times in life."

Years ago during my first visit to Munich, Germany, the colleague who had picked me up at the airport told me that he had already planned the next day. "I thought you'd probably want to go to Dachau," he said.

That startled me! I had forgotten that Dachau, the infamous Nazi concentration camp where tens of thousands were killed, was that close to Munich. The camp had basically been left open. Most of the buildings had been torn down. Only a few were rebuilt to give the visitor an idea of what the prison would have been like for those living there.

Today Dachau is primarily paths of concrete and stone. Yet you can still sense in its surroundings the despair of what the camp once was. Although a memorial chapel stands there now, Dachau represents the worst of what humanity is capable of and the worst of possible life experience.

One memorial area has pictures and comments from diaries of prisoners who were in the camp. But on the walls of Dachau are written the first four verses of Psalm 130: "Out of the depths I have cried to You, O Lord; Lord, hear my voice! Let Your ears be attentive to the voice of my supplications. If You, Lord, should mark iniquities, O Lord, who could stand? But there is forgiveness with You, that You may be feared."

Should the message of this Psalm of penitence reach even to Dachau? Yes, even Dachau! This concentration camp was the kind of experience that one identifies with in this Psalm. Yet Psalm 130 is also a classic in its description of true new life and redemption. Martin Luther called this a "Psalmi Paulini" — or a Psalm of Paul the apostle. It truly does have a New Testament-like expression. Luther made these comments about Psalm 130:

It is as if he should say I have learned by experience, O Lord, why there is mercy with Thee, and why thou mayest claim this title unto Thyself, that Thou art merciful and forgivest sins. For in that Thou shuttest all under free mercy, and leavest nothing to the merits and works of men, therefore Thou art feared. But if all things were not placed in Thy mercy, and we could take away our sins by our own strength, no man would fear Thee, but the whole world would proudly disregard Thee. For daily experience shows that where there is not this knowledge of God's mercy, men walk in the presumption of their own merits and righteousness. The true fear of God, the true worship, the true reverence, yea, the true knowledge of God rests on nothing but mercy, and through Christ we assuredly trust that God is reconciled unto us."[2]

Indeed this Psalm, beginning as it does out of the depths, rises to what is probably the clearest statement of New Testament Gospel found in the Old Testament.

Another writer concerning this Psalm said, "The psalmist wants to tell you that God is not just able to save us, but He saves us out of His abundance of mercy, and he has plenty left over for others. He has armloads of salvation."[3]

The Course of the Psalmist's Cry

It is so extremely important as we study this Psalm that we allow the Holy Spirit to help us understand and surrender our involvement in all the life experiences we walk through. Whatever they happen to be, we must surrender them to the Lord, trusting Him for true redemption. You see, redemption isn't just a spiritual work that takes place in our spirit. The redemption of our lives and our circumstances is a very practical thing.

Psalm 130 is basically divided into four simple two-verse stanzas. I believe the first stanza deals with importunate prayer; the second, with immediate forgiveness; and the third, with imperative patience. The fourth stands alone victoriously, providing insurmountable assurance.

In the total application of this Psalm, an imposing protection can come upon the reader's life. We will review this result at the end of this chapter. But for now, recognize that the *course* of the psalmist's cry is to answer the question, "How can you protect your fellowship with God?"

Begin at the Beginning

The opening words of the psalmist are heart-moving. Listen again to what he says: "Out of the depths I have cried to You, O Lord; Lord, hear my voice! Let Your ears be attentive to the voice of my supplications" (verses 1,2).

The circumstances behind this Psalm must not be overlooked. Most of us find such "depths" — whether mental, emotional, or physical — to be a place of depression. These depths can result from other people's actions toward ourselves or from self-imposed injury. But in whatever way these difficult experiences arrive in our lives, they are always something we hope to get out of or simply run from.

This psalmist declares, "It is out of the depths." The sentence construction in the Hebrew language means literally, "from the depths," or "as a result of the depths." The point here for us is very, very strategic to the ultimate outcome of our situation: We must learn to surrender our circumstances to the Lord.

One great missionary leader wrote a book out of the suffering of his own son. When his son was 14 years old, doctors discovered dangerous growths in his head. A series of surgeries followed — ordeals that involved not only hours of operations, but many hours of recovery in the midst of negative and disheartening predictions about his condition. This missions father wrote a book out of that experience entitled, *Please Don't Waste Your Suffering*. In his book, he related how he learned to surrender this painful situation to the Lord.

We must come to understand that God wants everything in our lives to progress toward greater understanding and revelation of His purpose. In order for that to happen, however, we must surrender to Him even the circumstances we face "out of the depths."

The Nature of Supplication

This Psalm also talks about the nature of our supplication. Several terms for supplication are used here, such as the word "cried": "Out of the depths I have *cried* to you..." (verse 1). Perhaps a better translation of "cried" is "I *invoke* you." The Hebrew word suggests the meaning of actually accosting someone — grabbing hold of him and not letting him go!

For instance, the blind man by the side of the road *cried* out, "...Jesus, thou Son of David, have mercy on me" (Mark 10:47 *KJV*). When the people pushed him down and said, "Hold your peace," the Bible says, "...he cried *the more a great deal*, Thou Son of David, have mercy on me" (verse 48 *KJV*)!

If we are to receive answers to our prayers, we must all learn the nature of true supplication. It is not a casual "Well, God, whatever Your will is, may it be so. Whatever You wish to do, Lord, may it happen according to Your promises."

There is a great gulf between supplication and that kind of lazy, halfhearted prayer. Jesus spent a lot of time teaching about prayer. Some of His teaching on this subject concerned how to make supplication to the Lord by developing *importunity* in prayer.

How can any of us forget Luke 11:9-13? The verbs in the original Greek demand that we translate these verses: "If you ask *and keep on asking* and if you knock *and keep on knocking,* the Lord will answer you. Just as a father would not give a serpent to a son who asks for bread, neither will the Father give evil to those who ask of Him the Holy Spirit" (author's paraphrase). What a specific teaching!

Earlier in Luke 11, Jesus taught on another aspect of prayer:

"...Which of you shall have a friend, and go to him at midnight and say to him, 'Friend, lend me three loaves;

'for a friend of mine has come to me on his journey, and I have nothing to set before him';

"and he will answer from within and say, 'Do not trouble me; the door is now shut, and my children are with me in bed; I cannot rise and give to you'?

"I say to you, *though he will not rise and give to him because he is his friend, yet because of his persistence he will rise* and give him as many as he needs.

Luke 11:5-8

Then in Luke 18, Jesus told a story about a widow who went before an unrighteous judge. The widow kept saying to the judge, "Avenge me of my adversary!" And do you know what the judge eventually said? "Look, I don't fear God, nor do I fear man." (Notice he did *not* say he didn't fear a woman!) "But this widow is troubling me, and I fear if I don't do something, she will weary me to death" (verses 1-5, author's paraphrase).

Then Jesus said, "And shall God not avenge His own elect who cry out day and night to Him, though He bears long with them?" (Luke 18:7). God is *not* an unrighteous judge, but how much more will He avenge those who are serious about making supplication to Him?

Take note of this: The Greek verb for "cry out" in Luke 18:7 corresponds to the Hebrew word "cry" in Psalm 130:1. In other words, Jesus is saying in Luke 18:7, "How much more will God avenge those who cry unto Him and *implore Him*?"

Perhaps our often casual attitude toward our faith is the reason we receive so little of God's blessings in life. We ask little; we believe little; and we really aren't even concerned whether it happens or not! "What will be, will be," we say, as we drift along in our careless Christian experience.

My last words may have stunned or offended you. Perhaps your response is "Speak for yourself!" But consider this: An importunate prayer comes from the most profound depths of the heart and from the innermost recesses of the mind. It comes with great fervor and with great earnestness of soul.

When Elijah prayed, he first sought a solitary place. Then when he had *placed his head between his knees* and stirred his heart to a state of great fervor, he began to pour forth his prayers until the answer came (1 Kings 18:42-45). Elijah wasn't distracted or yawning when he prayed that prayer; his heart was on fire with a great eagerness to receive his answer!

I have seen men and women praying thus from the depths of their hearts for a spouse or a child who was sick. I myself have had many such moments in my own prayer life — more often than not, I am ashamed to say, during the sunrise of my Christian experience.

I care that we know the difference between half-hearted prayer and fervent supplication! Our prayers so often return to us unanswered because we do not pray from the depths of our souls.

I include these thoughts from an old devotional (the source of which I have lost) because they speak so thoroughly of this issue:

He who prays out of the deep of his soul, even before he obtains what he prays for, receives good from his prayer; for it represses all the *perturbations* of his soul, quiets his anger, expels from his heart hatred, extinguishes desire, diminishes the love of things pertaining only to this life, and composing his soul in great tranquility, it ascends finally into heaven itself.

We are all like the psalmist — our life hangs upon the thread of divine compassion.

'There Is Forgiveness With You'

Obviously, Psalm 130 has already begun to dig deeply into our spirits. Now it continues: "If You, Lord, should mark iniquities, O Lord, who could stand? But there is forgiveness with You, that You may be feared" (Psalm 130:3,4). The word translated "mark" in verse 3 is later translated "watch" in verse 6 regarding "...those who watch for the morning." It is a Hebrew word meaning "keep" or "watch." Most notably it refers to "keeping in memory," perhaps in order to punish. It implies diligent observance and a kind of rigid, judicial and perpetual memory of what was done amiss.

It is certainly not a new thought, nor do we need to be reminded that all of us are sinners. We are all somewhat separated and out of touch with God. We may not have spent time behind bars, but we all have rather abysmal records for "doing the right thing."

I have mentioned the passage from Psalm 130 being written on the walls of Dachau. Certainly, we understand its application to this dark portion of man's history. The psalmist writes, "Out of the depths I have cried to You, O Lord..." (verse 1). Nevertheless, "...there is forgiveness with You..." (verse 4). Forgiveness for Dachau? Isn't that pushing the envelope?

Actually this is exactly where this Psalm belongs — wherever our cry of supplication goes forth, based on truth regarding ourselves and others. If we do not absorb the enormity of God's ability to forgive, our lifestyle becomes an impossible difficulty.

In Dr. Joyce Brothers' column, the following letter was published:[4]

> Dear Dr. Brothers, I did something terrible fifteen years ago and I have never been able to put it out of my mind. In a sense, I've paid a terrible price for my sins because I've never known complete happiness since. I can't even discuss it now, or put it on paper because I'm so ashamed. Can I ever come to terms with it, or must I live with it forever? It is ruining my life.

> T.K. wrote this letter to the columnist anonymously. We are all sinners. Were we to deny that, we'd be liars. But some of us are like T.K.; we can't ever come to terms with God's answer to sin. We often live without forgiveness for ourselves, nor do we extend forgiveness to others.

> I once heard about a farmer in South Texas who refused to go to the various agricultural seminars to which he was often invited. His stock answer was "I already know how to farm better than I'm farming!"

I understand that sentiment. I already know how to be a better Christian than I am. I am already very much aware of what is not true in my experience. I am aware of broken laws and issues in my life that are not correct. "If You, Lord, should mark iniquities, O Lord, who could stand? But there is forgiveness with You, that You may be feared" (Psalm 130:3,4).

Don't you agree with this psalmist? He says in essence, "Oh, Lord, if You were putting a microscope on my life; if You were keeping a list and checking it twice just to find out who is naughty or nice — if that were really who You are, there wouldn't be a hope in hell or Heaven for me!" This psalmist is saying something so incredible about the character of God, even though he is writing so many hundreds of years ago!

You see, Psalm 130 is one of the most confusing Psalms to identify as to authorship. Some scholars say it came out of the exile period. It could have been written by someone like Nehemiah, or it may well have been written by David. But hear this! Whenever this Psalm was written out of the depths of personal despair, it was written by someone who had more of an understanding of New Testament grace than some of us who are living on *this* side of the Cross. *This psalmist understood the character of God.*

Our culture seems to instill within us a performance orientation. We think we have to do certain things or perform to a certain level in order to be accepted or considered a success. Consequently, many of us live our lives with this awful feeling of inadequacy and impotency.

But this psalmist rises above this. "I have discovered God's character," he says. "He isn't a policeman. He isn't observing us under a microscope to see what iniquities are evident in our lives. If that were the case, we would have no hope! But our God is a God of infinite forgiveness!"

Please notice the phrase "...there is forgiveness with You...." The forgiveness is in God Himself. The fact that we can receive immediate forgiveness for our trespasses is not only a result of God's righteous character, but also because God has provided for forgiveness within *Himself*. Human merits are excluded from the whole scheme of salvation. Forgiveness is God's exclusive prerogative, flowing from His grace and the glory of His government.

The Direction Toward Fellowship

Again, I must give you these two verses in context: "Yahweh, if You were to take our iniquities into account, if You were to mark or observe us for our iniquities, no one could stand. But with You there is forgiveness, that You may be *feared*." (The word "feared" is how the *King James Version* translates it.)

Now, I'm not going to give you a simplistic explanation that says there are different Hebrew words for "fear" and "reverence." There aren't. Oh, there are Hebrew words for "fear" that are worse than this one, but this is the most frequently used word. It can be used to mean "absolute, terrified fear" or even "hysterical fear." However, its predominant use, as every Bible scholar will tell you, is *reverence* — specifically, *reverence in relationship*.

If I didn't know that from my own studies, I would know it from my experience with God Himself. God isn't trying to make us relate to Him in fear and trembling. He's trying to bring us into intimacy and relationship.

Nothing makes a Christian obedient in a car more quickly than a red or blue light flashing in their rear view mirror. Yet that kind of fear does *not* produce intimacy!

Do we think of God as a heavenly policeman who is always making a list and checking it twice? Do we think of Him as One who counts, "One, two, three — you're out!" Do we really believe that God gets up every morning to see how many kids He can kick out of the family? If these are our ideas of God, we will never know intimacy with Him!

"Lord, You don't *mark* iniquity. There's an abundance of forgiveness in You because You know it is the only way we can have intimacy. Intimacy with mankind was important enough to You for You to take care of the sin issue so You could be revered and loved."

It is impossible for me to describe my anguish for so many in the Church who live under the grace of God and through the Lord Jesus Christ, yet don't know any genuine peace. God put all sin away by one sacrifice. He doesn't even *see* sin anymore. It is already under the blood of Christ and atoned for, even for the whole world! Yet some still live with less peace and assurance than this psalmist had under the Old Covenant.

How was this psalmist able to obtain such peace? By his recognition of God's righteous character.

We desire to enter into true worship and to become more intimate with God. Yet so many of us are convinced that if God were just given a chance, He'd wipe us out as a result of last night's activities or something we did last week that wasn't pleasing to Him.

My friend, God wants your fellowship. Oh, He wants to be revered! So He points to you the way: "The fear of the Lord is the beginning of wisdom..." (Proverbs 9:10). If you fear God, you will depart from evil and hate iniquity. Remember, it's the kind of fear that is involved with *relationship*.

Personally, I would do anything to avoid harming my relationship with the Lord or violating the love and reverence I have for Him!

The Imperative Outcome of Patience and Peace

A third aspect in this Psalm is equally important — the outcome of patience and peace. The psalmist says, "I wait for the Lord, my soul waits, and in His word I do hope. My soul waits for the Lord more than those who watch for the morning — yes, more than those who watch for the morning" (Psalm 130:5,6).

The word "wait" used in this little stanza is very interesting. It is not the normal word for "wait," which basically means "to sit it out." I admit that, in this sense of the word, I wait very *im*patiently. I don't wait well at traffic lights, for my wife, etc. I'm not a good waiter in that regard at all.

But this word "wait" means "to bind something together" or "to twist, collect, or gather together." The word points to a specific purpose or direction. The psalmist is saying, "The process of my life experience is bringing me together. There's an integrity developing in my life, and that integrity has to do with a focus on Yahweh."

Do you expect something from me? You'll be disappointed. Anyone can find me in moments when I am not at my best — certainly not at my highest point of glorifying the Lord.

How about your local church? Are you expecting the church you attend to exhibit clear perfection?

Someone once said to me, "I don't go to church because there are hypocrites there."

I simply asked that person, "What other experiences do you exclude because there are hypocrites present? Do you stay out of hospitals because of hypocrites? Or do you refuse to buy groceries because of hypocrites?" In truth, what other experiences besides church *does* one decide to exclude from life because hypocrisy is present?

"I wait for the Lord; *He* is my direction, my expectation, and my focus." There is the answer. Only in *His Word* do I put my hope and my trust.

Obviously, this psalmist has moved beyond expectations of forgiveness into a way of life that is maintained in integrity. "My life is given integrity because my expectation is toward the Lord," he seems to write.

"I wait for the Lord to come into my experience. The foundation of His Word is where I place my hope." That is a statement of my future as well as of my past and present. "I am bound together with the Lord. My life is twisted together with His life into meaning and value as I wait upon Him."

The psalmist believed that God was gracious and forgiving. Out of that confidence sprang the hope that gave him patience and quieted him.

The Ultimate Goal
of Insurmountable Assurance

This Psalm ends in an insurmountable experience of assurance: "O Israel, hope in the Lord; for with the Lord there is mercy, and with Him is abundant redemption. And He shall redeem Israel from all his iniquities" (Psalm 130:7,8).

Here again the Lord Himself is given as the grounds for hope. Remember, the word "Lord" is actually *Yahweh*. Three times in this Psalm, the critical verses begin with the word *Yahweh*, even though *Elohim* is the more general word for "God" and *Adonai* is the frequently used word for "Lord." To the Hebrew mind, however, *Yahweh* is the unpronounceable name that speaks of the God whose nature is to create and bring life into existence. The God who was, who is, and who always will be!

Here the psalmist specifically says that the ground of his hope is in Yahweh's loyal covenant love — *love that keeps commitment in spite of everything*!

The word translated "mercy" is *hesed*, meaning "loyal love" or "covenant love." This is the kind of love that always reminds the beloved of its original hope and promise. *Hesed* is often translated "lovingkindness" and sometimes "mercy," but always it is a word that speaks about *covenant* and *faithfulness to a bond, a trust, or a relationship.*

Our relationship with God is based on the fact that He has declared something to be true; He has made a provision for us *in Himself*. However, after we enter a relationship with Him, we seem to continually fail and fall. Yet God *cannot* and *will not* break *His* covenant! It is as though the psalmist says, "I come to You, Lord. My hope for the future is in You, just as the forgiven sins of my past are in You. My hope for the future rests in the knowledge that You are always a loyal, loving, covenant-keeping God."

Our lives will inevitably be filled with people who break covenants with us. That's just the way it goes. Many times in our experience, people say to us, "I will never leave you; I will always be here for you." Yet many of us attest with great sorrow that sometimes people who made those commitments to us didn't keep them.

But when God says, "You are Mine; I will never leave nor forsake you," He isn't just talking about our *good* times. He's talking about *always, in every circumstance*. The covenant He has entered into with us is the basis of our hope for the future, and, of course, it is also the adequacy of our present provision.

I would translate these last two verses of Psalm 130 this way: "He will redeem Israel from all her iniquities because there is an abundance of redemption with Him." In the *King James Version*, "plenteous redemption" is the arresting phrase. Actually, it isn't just love in this passage — it is *steadfast* love. It isn't just redemption — it is *plenteous* redemption!

One of the translators says it this way: "His love is constant, and *He is always willing to save*."[5] *The Living Bible* paraphrases this verse: "He is loving and kind, and *comes to us with armloads of salvation*."[6]

If *that* isn't enough for you, let me give you the definition of "redemption" — a word that means "to set free; to set loose; and to *totally* provide for"!

Thus, we complete our walk through the four two-verse stanzas of Psalm 130. We watched the beginning of the psalmist's deep and troublesome experience. Yet we also witnessed an understanding of God that in the end changes everything we perceive about Him. What faith this psalmist possessed! He could see a day when God would redeem Israel of all its iniquities. Although this psalmist was surrounded by a religious system that required sacrifices for almost every occasion, he saw something so much deeper in the character of God.

Imposing Protection:
How To Protect Your Fellowship With God

The teachings of the 130th Psalm are unique on the subject of an imposing protection. A quick review of what we have studied becomes a syllabus on maintaining and protecting our fellowship with God.

This psalmist cries out to the Lord in the midst of his deepest despair. This tells us that a deep, serious, continuing life of prayer is our greatest protection. The psalmist prays, "...Let your ears be attentive to the voice of my supplication." Yet we know that prayer is not only the act of supplicating, interceding, or asking. Prayer is also a two-way conversation that arises from a loyal, continued, and deep mutual commitment. This mutual commitment becomes our guarantee that God will use everything at His disposal to keep our lives on target. Thus, when prayer vanishes from our experience, we are open to the horrendous loss that comes with broken fellowship.

But Psalm 130 also speaks of a clear, specific understanding of the believer's position and of sin's payment. We must live in acceptance of the fact that Jesus once and for all put away sin by the offering of Himself (Hebrews 9:25,26). We also need to understand what Colossians 2:13 and 14 means:

> **And you, being dead in your trespasses and the uncircumcision of your flesh, He has made alive together with Him, having forgiven you all trespasses,**
>
> *having wiped out the handwriting of requirements that was against us, which was contrary to us. And He has taken it out of the way, having nailed it to the cross.*

No one can ever enter into God's fullness until they accept what His Word says!

"You mean, Jesus took care of the sin I haven't yet committed?"

Yes, it was nailed there to the Cross. It is under the blood of Jesus Christ.

"You mean, the ungodly are already forgiven?"

Yes. That is what Paul declares when he says, "For when we were still without strength, in due time Christ died for the ungodly" (Romans 5:6). Christ's death was not based on what the ungodly have done; it was based on what *He* has done. Now, of course, people must accept that reconciliation. But *He is already reconciled to them* (2 Corinthians 5:17-21).

You need to understand what these scriptures say. *That's the only way to obtain continuing peace in your life.*

Third, in order to protect our fellowship and relationship with God, we must resist condemnation at all costs.

Please note that condemnation and genuine conviction are not the same things. The devil is the author of condemnation. He comes to your mind, taunting, "Look at your life. How could you do this? Look at how you are now. God isn't pleased with that! How can you claim to be a Christian? You should never take Communion."

These are all lying obscenities of Satan, who always brings condemnation. If you listen to the devil rather than the Lord, you will never enjoy an intimate relationship with the Lord.

The Word says, "There is therefore now no condemnation to those who are in Christ Jesus, who do not walk according to the flesh, but according to the Spirit" (Romans 8:1). *The voice of condemnation can only be the voice of the enemy, the devil.*

A fourth requirement for protecting your fellowship with God is that you confess your sins quickly and thoroughly. Don't let the bill mount up! Keep your heart clean and free. You'll find that repentance — breathing out the stagnant air and breathing in fresh, invigorating life — is the most wonderful thing in the world.

Run to the Lord with confession. Be quick and thorough; let nothing come in between the transgression and your confession of sin to the Lord. Remember, the forgiveness has already been given. You are simply to confess your sins, agreeing with God (1 John 1:9).

Another important step in protecting our fellowship with God is to develop a strong reverence for Him, which includes a hatred for sin and its effects. Our greatest protection comes from developing a holy horror of anything that would break our relationship with God. Reverence for God produces the highest and most intense desire for intimacy with the Lord. When we possess this kind of fervent desire for intimacy, we will hate anything that could trouble or in any way cause our relationship with the Lord to be compromised.

Sixth, we are to protect our fellowship with God by developing a strong, resilient love of His Word. Years ago, my godly father wrote in an early Bible he gave me, "This book will keep you from sin, or sin will keep you from this book." I could never forget those words. When the Word of God becomes dry or unimportant to me, I know I need a thorough spiritual check-up.

Finally, if we are to apply the imposing protection available to us, we must accept and live courageously in the relationship of covenant. The author of Psalm 130 has given us abundant encouragement about the covenant-keeping, merciful love and commitment of God. We must never be persuaded to drop our confidence in that truth.

To the staggering early Hebrew Christians, the New Testament author wrote, "Let us hold fast the confession of our hope without wavering, for He who promised is faithful" (Hebrews 10:23). We all need to be constantly reminded of that divine admonition!

Checkmate or One More Move?

I am not a stranger to the strange, inexplicable cycles of depression and despondency. I understand depression in ways some people know nothing about. My wife, Anita, can spot those waves while they are still forming offshore, so to speak.

In those kinds of moments, you *can't* depend on a change of feelings because they often don't change. You can't just wait until the depression lifts because it often doesn't lift. In fact, if your depression is anything like mine, the more you acknowledge it, the deeper it gets. It is like a thick fog that rolls in off the coast in San Francisco.

So what can you do? You can stand on the basis of the complete authoritative, unchanging Word of God. Don't emphasize how you feel. Focus on what *God* says. *Hang on to His promises with tenacity.*

I am so grateful that someone, perhaps a Sunday school teacher, got through to me very early in my life that it is only *the Word* that really counts, not our feelings or emotions.

So when the enemy comes in like a flood, stand upon God's Word. You are accepted in the Beloved. You are God's perfection. You stand in His strength!

A story is told of a painting depicting Faust — the same Faust who gambled with his soul. The painting shows a game of chess, with Faust at one side of the board and Satan at the other. In the painting, the game is almost over, and Faust has only a few chess pieces left to play — a king, a knight, and two pawns. On his face is a look of blank, yet feverish despair. At the other side of the board, the devil leers in anticipation of his coming triumph. For many years, chess players and others looked carefully at the painting and agreed that Faust's position was hopeless — *checkmate* was certain.

One day into the art gallery came a true master of the game of chess. He, too, stood gazing for a long time at the painting. He was fascinated by the despair on the face of Faust. As he stood there, the chess master began to immerse himself into the actual game as shown in the painting, carefully studying the pieces on the board. Then the light broke. The rather crowded gallery was startled by the loud shout from the master: *"It's a lie! The king and the knight have another move!"*

That is exactly what the New Testament Gospel is all about. Satan is always coming into your life, saying, "Checkmate! Nothing else can happen; this is it. You have blown your opportunity. There can be no new agenda for you. You have blown your chance to do the will of God. There's nothing else."

And many of us, like the casual onlookers who strolled through that museum, look at our own lives and agree with the devil: "That's right! That's the story of my life. Checkmate."

But then, thank God, someone comes along to contradict us! Often it is the Master, the God of loving provision Himself. He says to us, "Satan is a liar. There is still a move left that you can take. That move begins with repentance. Then comes forgiveness, restoration, new life and renewed intimacy. There *is* a way to change this scenario. There is a move left!"

When I ponder my own life experience, I often think of Psalm 130:1: "Out of the depths I have cried to You, O Lord." Out of my own "depths" experience, I came to the Lord. From that act, an image of God has developed in my heart that is far above what religious people tell me is possible! I have come into an experience with a living God who keeps covenant; who is full of forgiveness; and whose character is not one "to mark" iniquities. I have found such a wonderful place of intimacy and reverence through relationship!

Perhaps Satan has tried to lie to you that you are checkmated and that this is the limitation you will always have to live with. It's just the way life is going to be. Well, this psalmist wants you to know that God is able to set you free. He will redeem even the circumstances you face.

Never accept a lie! New life and new beginnings are available to you! There is a resurrection in store for you because of who God is, what He has done, what His character will forever be. Just allow the Grand Master to show you the moves that will bring you out of any checkmated position in which you find yourself!

Finally, let me suggest a prayer you can pray at the end of this study:

Father, I have great thanksgiving in the presence of Your covenant-keeping love. I am astonished at such love, overwhelmed by Your care. Help me to always be able to hear Your voice, even in the midst of despair. Lead me into all paths of Your truth. Produce in me a quickened desire to walk in the fulfillment of Your purposes for my life. Through Jesus Christ, my Lord and Redeemer, Who has answered my every cry in the night. Amen.

PSALM 143

Seventh of the Penitential Psalms

Fitly do the Penitential Psalms end with these words; for the final end, the great purpose, the eternal result of penitence is to make us GOD'S servants. If at the end of our penitence, if at the end of our life, we can say these words, "I am Thy servant," it will be enough, it will be the passport to heaven.1

— Alfred G. Mortimer
Notes on the Seven Penitential Psalms

CHAPTER 7

The Believer's Central Issue of Despair

Psalm 143

$\mathscr{P}$SALM *143*

An earnest appeal for guidance and deliverance. A Psalm of David.

Hear my prayer, O Lord, give ear to my supplications! In Your faithfulness answer me, and in Your righteousness.

Do not enter into judgment with Your servant, for in Your sight no one living is righteous.

For the enemy has persecuted my soul; he has crushed my life to the ground; he has made me dwell in darkness, like those who have long been dead.

Therefore my spirit is overwhelmed within me; my heart within me is distressed.

I remember the days of old; I meditate on all Your works; I muse on the work of Your hands.

I spread out my hands to You; my soul longs for You like a thirsty land. Selah

Answer me speedily, O Lord; my spirit fails! Do not hide Your face from me, lest I be like those who go down into the pit.

Cause me to hear Your lovingkindness in the morning, for in You do I trust; cause me to know the way in which I should walk, for I lift up my soul to You.

Deliver me, O Lord, from my enemies; in You I take shelter.

Teach me to do Your will, for You are my God; your Spirit is good. Lead me in the land of uprightness.

Revive me, O Lord, for Your name's sake! For Your righteousness' sake bring my soul out of trouble.

In Your mercy cut off my enemies, and destroy all those who afflict my soul; for I am Your servant.

What is the critical issue of despair that threatens to overtake a spiritual Christian? It is certainly not his own personal discomfort, nor worry about the end of the world.

I believe I can answer from my own heart as vulnerably as possible. The crucial issue of despair for me is that my weaknesses; my potential for failure or sin; or even the direct attack of my enemy will keep me from achieving God's fullest purpose in my life. That is the cause of the spiritual despair with which I sometimes struggle.

This is not an issue every Christian struggles with, but *it is THE issue for those who have a unique sense of God's destiny upon them.* Their concern becomes not that their lives might end or that they might have to endure pain as a part of life. Instead, they are primarily concerned that somehow their lives will be *cut short* by their own sinfulness or by the work of the enemy.

The Last of the Psalms of Penitence

Our study in Psalm 143 ends our study of the Penitential Psalms. As we have discovered, these seven Psalms are unique among the 150 Psalms of the Bible. They are a textbook in themselves, not only because of their confessional nature, but because they have become the text of penitence for the Early Church from the second century. There is even historical reason to believe that Israel itself used these seven Psalms in their own special times of worship that included repentance and supplication.

David didn't write *all* the Penitential Psalms, let alone all the Psalms in general. Nevertheless, the spirit of David pervades the entire book of Psalms. His appointed worship team, the family of Asaph, wrote a whole group of the Psalms. Others who were directly related to David's family contributed as well to the book of Psalms.

Campbell McAlpine, a good friend of mine from England, recently reminded me that David is mentioned 1,300 times in Scripture, far more than any other non-divine person. Seventy of those references to David are in the New Testament, even though he was an Old Testament character.

In Matthew 1:1, David is the first name mentioned after Jesus. And in the book of Revelation, the last book of the New Testament, he is the last name mentioned by our Lord, who said, "...I am the Root and the Offspring of David..." (Revelation 22:16). Perhaps the frequency that David's name is referenced is meant to encourage all of us!

Psalm 143 is unique, not only because it is the seventh of the Penitential Psalms, but because it is in its own way a conclusion. One writer very cleverly said, "It has been regarded as the last of a series of penitential psalms...They represent seven rungs on the ladder of repentance, this last one being a prayer against the Last Judgment (Psalm 143:2)."[2]

Let us be reminded that repentance is always a process. It is never just a crisis or an emotion, but always an ongoing experience.

The last of the Penitential Psalms has a superscription above it, as do many of the Psalms. In many language translations overseas, the superscription is counted as the first verse. I have always believed that the superscriptions should be intensely studied.

This superscription says, "An earnest appeal for guidance and deliverance. A Psalm of David." The *Septuagint*, a Greek translation, reads, "A Psalm of David written while fleeing from his son, Absalom."

Some modern teachers think that because of the construction of Psalm 143 and its quotations from other Psalms, it must have been written at a later time. However, our purpose is not to argue about theories. This psalmist is in a truly dark moment of the soul. Perhaps he has spent an actual night in the temple, awaiting a word to come from the priests in the morning, for he prays, "Let me hear in the morning the word of Your covenant love" (verse 8, author's paraphrase).

The psalmist is like a prisoner in a holding tank, awaiting a verdict. Perhaps it really is David on the night he fled Jerusalem, running from Absalom — unable to sleep, waiting to see what the morning would bring.

> **Hear my prayer, O Lord, give ear to my supplications! In Your faithfulness answer me, and in Your righteousness.**
>
> **Do not enter into judgment with Your servant, for in Your sight no one living is righteous.**
>
> **For the enemy has persecuted my soul; he has crushed my life to the ground; he has made me dwell in darkness, like those who have long been dead.**
>
> **Therefore my spirit is overwhelmed within me; my heart within me is distressed.**
>
> **Psalm 143:1-4**

The Problem

There are two basic problems presented in Psalm 143 — the same two problems that most of us face in life. First, it is clear from the first two verses that the psalmist understands his own sin. He says, "Do not enter into judgment with Your servant, for in Your sight no one living is righteous" (verse 2). He understands his own failures and weaknesses that are preventing the fulfillment of God's purpose for his life.

The apostle Paul develops much of his viewpoint in New Testament theology from passages like this Psalm, as seen by comparing verse 2 with two scriptures from the Pauline epistles:

> **...By the works of the law no flesh shall be justified.**
>
> **Galatians 2:16**

> **Therefore by the deeds of the law no flesh will be justified in His sight, for by the law is the knowledge of sin.**
>
> **Romans 3:20**

There is no hope if God judges any of us based simply upon our performance. We would never come through with a passing grade!

Clearly, this is the first problem the psalmist must face, for he is himself a weak, stumbling, failing and sinning believer. But besides this difficulty, he now faces another problem that isn't traceable to his own failure.

This psalmist has real enemies — people and events that persecute his soul and crush his life to the ground. These circumstances bring him distress and afflict his spirit, causing him to dwell in a dark moment. The psalmist must therefore deal with both issues: 1) the limitations he imposes on himself, and 2) the limitations placed on him by others' actions over which he has no control. Such is the dilemma of every Christian today as well.

I believe when you carefully study this seventh Penitential Psalm, you will discover that the real issue from the writer's viewpoint (as almost every scholar agrees) is not fear of the Lord's judgment; rather, it is this psalmist's overwhelming fear that he will be cut off before *he completes God's purpose in his life*. His overriding concern is that he will fail in his covenant responsibility.

This agony is revealed most often through words expressing a fear of broken intimacy or a fear of a disturbed purpose. This is the real issue rather than any worry about self-destruction.

We must all hear this carefully because it is the highest level of *penitence* that exists. It is not penitence because we are sorry for our sin, nor even penitence because we know that God has been affected by our sin. It is the highest level of penitence, in which we view our lives as God does, perceiving the difference between what He intends our lives to be versus what they have become.

"I need help; otherwise, my life and my spirit will fail," the psalmist declares in verse 7 (author's paraphrase). Later in that same verse, he states in effect, "I long for intimacy; do not hide Your face from me lest I be like those who go down into the pit of death."

The psalmist here declares that without intimacy — without achieving what God intends for him — he might as well be dead. He further expresses that he even needs to be reminded of the covenant love of God. He needs to remember that it is God's will he wants and that he must know the way he should walk (verses 5-8). "Teach me Your will," he prays. "Help me walk on level ground" (author's paraphrase).

Only later in verse 11 does the psalmist really talk about survival: "Revive me, O Lord, for Your name's sake! For Your righteousness' sake bring my soul out of trouble." Even here the issue is not strength to live more days! Why live more days if those days are not going to be fruitful and valuable?

"Give me strength to be the servant of Yours I am supposed to be," the writer essentially prays. "Give me the strength to fulfill the purpose You have destined for my life."

An Example From the Sinless One

Unlike the psalmist in Psalm 143, Jesus our Lord had no sin in His life. Jesus also had no overwhelming and distressing sense of his own failure. Nonetheless, the results of His life still crushed in upon Him! His human (although not moral) weakness came like a flood upon His life as well. The New Testament book of Hebrews tells us that Jesus feared what this psalmist feared namely, that His life would be prematurely ended. Let us review these words:

> Who [Jesus], in the days of His flesh, when He had offered up prayers and supplications, with vehement cries and tears to Him who was able to save Him from death, and was heard because of His godly fear,
>
> though He was a Son, yet He learned obedience by the things which He suffered.
>
> **Hebrews 5:7,8**

Jesus wished to *complete* the purpose He earnestly believed the Father had given Him. That is really what the agony of Gethsemane was all about! Jesus was certainly not merely struggling with a fear of death or a fear of the Roman guards and Jewish leaders. Jesus agonized for *completion*; He petitioned for *resurrection*. He prayed that He would be able to complete His task.

Jesus supplicated against anything that would prematurely end his servanthood short of its accomplishment. The Father answered that prayer. Jesus faced His enemies with overwhelming assurance. He experienced the failure of His friends with incomprehensible forgiveness. Later He walked through the horrors and embarrassment of His own tortures and death with dignity and strength.

Satan *couldn't* take Jesus' life — He laid it down! Death was not the victor; it was the vanquished. Hell could not conquer; it was *invaded*. Jesus prayer was answered! He finished His task. From the Cross He cried, *"Tetellesthai."* This is the Greek exclamation for "It is now complete" or "It is finished!"

That indeed must be the underlying prayer of each of us who are believers. Whatever difficulties we face, whether self-imposed or the results of our enemies, we *must* finish our course.

Some Christians die before their time. Still others surrender to despondency, discouragement, and debilitation. They live out their lives paralyzed as useless victims.

Many of us are often like this psalmist, possessing an overwhelming awareness of our sinfulness and our inadequacy. We say, "I am God's servant, and yet I am unrighteousness. I wouldn't stand a moment if God entered a judgment against me. I'm undone; I'm unclean. And what's more, I'm overwhelmed and crushed by my enemies!"

The Psalmist's Answer to the Quandary

So what do we do when we have allowed our spirits to be overcome and driven to consternation? What do we do when, like the psalmist in Psalm 143:4, we are driven to numbness?

I believe this psalmist answers our quandary in two specific ways. These two solutions are easier to find than in any of the other Penitential Psalms.

First, the psalmist suggests some interim spiritual commitments to make during times of *delay*. These are "practice commitments" to help you prepare for the moment of danger. When no great victory seems to be imminently forthcoming, you hang on with these "in-the-meantime" commitments. The second answer this psalmist suggests includes specific points of intercession that will release God's ultimate purpose.

So there we have it: 1) some things we can hold on to when holding on is all we can do; and 2) some clear points of intercession to change the circumstances themselves.

Remember the Victories

The interim spiritual commitments our psalmist suggests may at first seem elementary. But when applied, they become a great help to us in moments of sheer survival. First, he writes, "I remember the days of old..." (verse 5). The Hebrew actually translates, "I *mark out*, or *recognize*, the days of old."

Do what God instructed the Israelites to do when they came out of Egypt: Put "piles of memorial stones" at places of great victories. Then when you start doubting in the midst of your present circumstances, go back to the pile of stones and remember what God has done for you in the past.

That is exactly what the psalmist is saying in verse 5. "I know something I can do even in times of delay, even during the most difficult trial. I can *remember*. I can journey back to a victory in my past that reminds me that God wants victory for me *today*."

May I share a similar personal moment from my own life? I attended a fine liberal arts college in Pennsylvania with a religious foundation (as is often the case in the United States). But as a result of many areas of study during my first two years, as well as involvement with my peers, I began to question the work of the Holy

Spirit that had been the overriding influence in my life as I was growing up.

I began to wonder if that work was more attributable to emotion and immaturity than to God. Particularly in question was the night God called me to the ministry at the age of 15 while attending a Christian high school in Georgia.

My academic and social success in this college was causing highly placed teachers to push me toward various careers as they sincerely cautioned me against "wasting" my life in ministry. I was deeply troubled.

Finally, as summer approached, I gathered money to make a special trip from Pennsylvania to Georgia. My trip could last a few days since both my current college and my former high school were between sessions.

When I arrived in Georgia, I met with old friends and told them my purpose for coming. They did not chide or preach to me. They said, "Take your time — look around. If what you had was real, you'll find your own reminders."

I went to the very classroom where late at night I had experienced my dynamic encounter with God and received His purpose for my life. The classroom was largely unchanged. Nevertheless, I moved the chairs as I had that night almost five years before. I knelt as close as I could remember to my "spot of Ebenezar."[3] Suddenly, I was washed over by an overwhelming reassurance of God's Presence and of my call.

Does God only speak in Georgia? Couldn't I have experienced renewal in my dorm in Pennsylvania? You already know the answer to those questions.

But like the psalmist, I had to mark a moment — remember a truth — during a time when everything about my life was up for grabs. I took the time to remember the days of old. It was an interim commitment I could make until the fog lifted and other things became more clear.

Meditate on His Works

The second interim commitment from the psalmist of Psalm 143 is also found in verse 5: "...I *meditate* on all Your works...." You could also translate this: "I *murmur* about Your works."

Please understand this clearly. The psalmist is not speaking here of God's workmanship or activities of creation. He is talking about meditating on God's *acts* in history. So we could translate the word "works" as "Your habitual practices."

The psalmist is saying, "I go over and over again in my mind about the way *God always works in people's lives.* I think about the way He always manifests His compassion and forgiveness in every situation. This is what I meditate on when I'm going through difficult times."

Malachi 3:16 is a wonderful scripture that reveals the importance of meditating on God and His works: "Then those who feared the Lord spoke to one another, and the Lord listened and heard them; so *a book of remembrance was written before Him for those who fear the Lord and who meditate on His name.*"

Oh, friend, please take note. A book of remembrance wasn't written for those who knew the score of a recent football game. It was written for those who love to meditate on and mention the works of the Lord — His faithfulness and His compassion!

These interim commitments continue in verse 5 with the psalmist saying, "...I muse [or *ponder*] on the work of Your hands." Here the focus is on that which

God has actually created and finished. Creation is the workmanship of God! We need to think about the wonderful things God does and *has* done.

'Spread Out Your Hands' to God in Prayer

After this the psalmist says, "I spread out my hands to you…" (Psalm 143:6). This verb is a declarative perfect, yet in a present tense. Again, we might translate this phrase, "I pray and I *continue* to pray. I continue to spread myself before You, Lord." (The Hebrews frequently stood with their hands raised when they prayed.) "My soul longs, it actually thirsts for You like a thirsty land." Eugene Peterson's translation, *The Message Bible*, reads, "…as a thirsty desert thirsting for rain."[4]

So the psalmist talks to himself; he mutters; he recognizes the history of a people who have lived under the rule of a faithful God. Then he begins remembering God's work in history and the power of His creative work, and he starts to get excited. He becomes emboldened! Now he stretches out his hand, longing for intimacy. He begins to taste victory!

When faced with adversity, you, too, must make a choice: You can sit all day long in your prison cell, moping and in despair, counting the bars on your cell door. Or, like Paul and Silas, you can turn a prison sentence into a prayer and praise meeting (Acts 16:16-40)! *It is entirely up to you.*

If you choose the latter option, there will be times when you don't go on the offensive. It may be a time of delay or denial; you may be in the despondency of failure or faced with the enemy's attack. But regardless of the circumstance, when you are *in between the problem and the manifested promise,* you simply stand your ground. Meditate on the works of God; muse on the works of His hand; and stretch forth your hands to Him based on His righteous character.

That's what you do in between!

Intercessory Prayers

The psalmist must eventually move from the interim spiritual commitments of verses 5 and 6. This was merely holding ground — a time of construction for the ultimate foundation of victory. Therefore, he quickly moves from hanging on during delay to praying some very specific prayers.

Granted, this is not an intercessory prayer book to pass out to a youth group. These are specific prayers for the kind of believer who understands his weaknesses and his enemy, but above all else understands and cries out for his divine purpose to be fulfilled.

The first of this psalmist's actual intercessions is based on an overwhelming awareness of his mortality and his weakness. "...My spirit is overwhelmed within me...," he cries (Psalm 143:4). Then at the end of this prayer, he prays, "Answer me speedily, O Lord, my spirit fails..." (verse 7). In the literal Hebrew, he prays, "I am at the end; I am nigh to perishing."

It seems close to the end, and this psalmist seems close to being destroyed. He further writes in verse 7, "...lest I be like those that go down into the pit *[a synonym for death]*." Without God's intervention, he earnestly believes that his ordeal will only end with his premature death.

I do not believe that this is just a prayer about wanting more days to live. Does this psalmist want more days to waste, more days to consume, more days to flitter away? No, I believe he cries out to finish something God has assigned to him. "Answer me speedily...!" he cries. The word "speedily" actually suggests "suddenly, like a flood." He's praying, "Please hurry up, God!"

This first specific intercession is extremely *importunate*. The psalmist is grabbing hold of the altar, and his prayer is based on a strategic awareness of limitations. You see, *godly people are pressed for time*. There is so much to do, so many limitations.

The psalmist is saying, "I see my own foolishness; I have an overwhelming sense of my own weakness. But the enemy's strategy is also coming against my life. Before I am finished doing the task I've been given, this thing called life is going to end. So speedily, Lord, answer me!"

In Genesis 15, Abraham wanted to know how he could fulfill the covenant purpose of God. How would he ever give birth to that promised son through whom the nations of the world were to be blessed?

"How will it happen?" he asked the Lord (Genesis 15:2,3).

God answered, "Make a sacrifice" (Genesis 15:9).

In obedience, Abraham cut the sacrifice and laid out the pieces of heifer, goat, ram, and several birds upon the sand. But suddenly *vultures* came to devour his sacrifice. This is a type and shadow of what I have seen often happening when men and women lay out their lives as a sacrifice for God. The vultures come and try to eat huge pieces of the flesh of their divine purpose!

I don't think Abraham used boxing gloves; nonetheless, a real fight ensued! "That's my sacrifice! Satan, you will not have that which was a sacrifice to Almighty God!"

There is a significant verse that is probably marked in every Bible I own. It is from the writings of Paul in Second Timothy 4:17: "But the Lord stood with me and strengthened me, so that *the message might be preached fully through me,* and that all the Gentiles might hear. And I was delivered out of the mouth of the lion."

Godly, spiritually awake believers know that the purpose of their lives is found in the purposes of God. They know they must stand with diligence and perseverance against anything or anyone who would shorten or abort that purpose.

This psalmist is determined to finish all four quarters of the game. He is going to fight all fifteen rounds; he will play to the last out of the ninth inning.

You should be aware of how important this type of intercession is. This is the difference between the "roll-over-in-defeat Christian" ("Pity me; this is the way it is") and the interceding Christian who strives for the fulfillment of God's purposes.

One translation of Psalm 143:11 reads, " For thy name's sake, O Lord, *preserve* my life."[6] *So quit engineering your own defeat! Don't yield to the pessimism of the enemy's lies!* As the old saying goes, "It's not over until the fat lady sings!" There is still plenty of time for you to see God's purpose fulfilled in your life. All Heaven awaits *your* response.

Remembrance

The second issue of intercession comes from the psalmist's overwhelming awareness of his forgetfulness. Perhaps this is the most pastoral point I can make from a study of Psalm 143.

This psalmist is aware that when depression, despondency, and discouragement arrives or when delay accumulates, the truth becomes less clear. He cries out, "Cause me to hear Your lovingkindness..." (Psalm 143:8). Once again, "lovingkindness" is the word *hesed*, meaning "covenant love" or "loyal love." Therefore, this verse could be translated, "Cause me to hear about Your loyal love in the morning." In other words, the psalmist is praying, "Reveal Your face, Lord, that I might trace out and become intimately acquainted with Your countenance. Remind me of Your covenant."

Darkness in the human spirit is a very real thing. I am not going to say that every Christian experiences it. But I *will* say that some Christians — generally those who are most sensitive and, in many instances, those upon whom God has placed His highest demands — will experience times when depression tries to move in.

When this happens, truth in the human spirit can become distorted into a kind of darkness. Condemnation can dim God's countenance as the accuser tries to blur the believer's understanding about the very basis of his salvation.

The phrase, "Cause me to hear" in verse 8 is actually a Hebrew phrase that means "contend with me; plead with me; strive with me." The phrase "to hear" comes from a Hebrew word that isn't a common word for registering sound on the eardrum. It is instead a word that means "let me hear *intelligently*; let me *discern* this truth; let me be attentive to it."

In effect, the psalmist is saying, "This despondency, this depression, this weakness of my spirit has distorted truth. Lord, You must *contend* with me. You have to be willing to plead with my spirit if I am to be reminded of Your covenant love.

"The enemy has slurred my speech and erased my memory. Please get serious with me. Contend with my depressed spirit, and bring intelligent awareness to my despondency. Help me perceive *again* the true conditions of Your loyal love. Teach me about the unconditional commitment You have made to me. Teach me about Your faithfulness and trace out the beauty of Your countenance upon my hand. Show me Your truth."

Now, that's a prayer of intercession! Again, it isn't a schoolboy's prayer. This is a person who is being tried in the midst of extremely difficult circumstances — more difficult than most Christians will ever face. He has an overwhelming sense of his own weakness and a heightened sense of the enemy of God's very purpose in his life.

Direction

The third of these intercessory prayers is also specific. It is an earnest plea for *clear direction*.

Each of us knows that the enemy works best in the midst of confusion. To divide and conquer is always his motive. The battle is very real, so every believer must know where he is going. In the second part of verse 8, the psalmist requests, "...Cause me to know the way in which I should walk...." Later in verse 10, he continues, "Teach me to do Your will...."

Further, the psalmist prays, "...Lead me in the way of uprightness." In the Hebrew, this suggests "Put me on a level path." This last phrase suggests that the psalmist is pleading to be led somewhere where the ground is level.

Again, a paraphrase is helpful: "God, my life is too valuable and important to waste. Contend with me. I'm dull; persuade me. You know everything about me, so reveal to me perfectly — not just Your will, but my every footstep.

"Lord, I'm childish. It takes the simplest diversion to make me stumble. Please lead me on level ground. Help me avoid that which is uneven. I'm so given to stumbling and falling. I am not ready for precipitous climbing yet. I am not a spiritual athlete. If You will, please clear out the way and walk me down to a spring meadow somewhere where it is safe. *I need a walk in the park for a while.*"

You have probably felt that way at one time or another. Again, however, I am very aware of a difference among Christians. On any given Sunday morning, there are many people who come to church by choice, yet who have still not come to understand their value or the critical nature of life in the Kingdom of God. On the other hand, many others walk in a constant sense of God's desire and purpose for their lives. That's the place of the most intense battle within and without.

I am often aware of that battle in myself. This psalmist wants us to be aware of it in him.

Perhaps as you have read these words, you know this intercessory prayer is most necessary for you. Your heart may be saying, "Lord, I need 'a walk in the park' for a while. I am stumbling around like a drunkard. I need someplace to go in my walk with You where there is no possibility of my stumbling. Please lead me to a level place. Build some confidence in me."

Protection

Next, the psalmist intercedes on the basis of *rightful protection.* Experts in the language of origin who study this Psalm tell us that, technically, it was written in the actual language a vassal would use toward his lord.

You see, in those days, vassals or bondservants often farmed the land. These vassals had committed themselves to a relationship with the lord who owned the land. The vassal gave produce to the lord, and the lord owed the vassal protection.

The language that is used here is very interesting. The psalmist tells the Lord, "…You are my God…" (verse 10), or, in other words, "You are my Patron, and I am Your servant."

Then the psalmist becomes combatant and goes on the offensive. "I'm on God's side," he says. "He's my Patron, my Protector. We have a relationship." It is as if the psalmist says, "I'll tell you one thing, devil. When you take me on, you take on my elder Brother!"

Let me ask you — do you believe that? Do you understand that? As a believer, you, too, can stand in the face of the devil and say, "Come on at me; I dare you, devil! Jesus will enjoy this fight!"

The psalmist continues in verse 9, "Deliver me, Lord, from my enemies…." Then he says in verse 12, "In Your mercy [*Your covenant or Your loyal love*] cut off [*put to an end*] my enemies, and destroy all those who afflict my soul; for I am Your servant." In other words, "Sic 'em, Jesus!"

Believe this: Despondency, depression, weakness, and death don't have a chance when a Christian takes his stand on the covenant of God and says, "I'm included in God. When you take me on, you tackle the hosts of Heaven. Go ahead, devil, because I am a servant. I am a vassal of the King of Heaven!" That kind of stance moves everything into an entirely different framework. This stance is *on the offensive*; it is the framework of intercession.

Power and Quickened Life

Although these last two things the psalmist prays for are taken out of order, I believe you will understand my purpose. The psalmist in this Psalm teaches a specific intercessory prayer about power and a quickened life, found in verse 11: "Revive me, O Lord, for Your name's sake! For Your righteousness' sake bring my soul out of trouble." The psalmist is telling the Lord, "It isn't enough that I know what You want me to do and where You want me to walk. I know who I am; but, Lord, You must also give me strength if I am even going to exist."

You will never know how many times I have stood on these words in verse 11 as I have traveled to 80-plus nations to preach the Gospel; stayed many times in very basic accommodations; and often used the most elementary means of travel. I have prayed, "Lord, I am Your servant. I am where You have placed me. Everything about this situation seems to be negative and death-bringing, but I stand on the basis of Your covenant. I want my story to be finished!"

It is our privilege to be like Jesus in negative situations (although, sadly, many of us don't take advantage of that privilege). We are to come to the Father and say, "I see what is coming, and I am not afraid of death. But *I don't want one day to be lost until I have finished what You have called me to do.* I want to be able to cry out on the other side of the experience that what You assigned me to do is done!

"That's why I pray to You in the bonds of this affliction, Lord. I ask that You would bring me forth. I need revival. I am at the point of death, weak to the point of ultimate weariness." What a specific intercession and supplication this makes!

Summary

This psalmist is talking about an *attitude* toward life. This attitude may seem strange to some. To them, it is odd that a man wouldn't be concerned about just living longer or building more, accumulating millions to leave for his children.

But this man pleads for a life to be lived on the sharp edge of finishing God's purpose for his life. Here is a man thoroughly and emotionally aware of his own weaknesses. He is acutely aware that in one moment of time, God's purpose could be ended in his life because of his own wrong choices. He is also aware of the effect and power of an enemy whose goal is to make sure his divine purpose in life remains unfulfilled. Therefore, this is a prayer that comes out of the heart of someone who understands how valuable he or she is to the bigger picture of God's plan!

I hope no one reading these words sees himself as a number or as something to be used or abused by someone else.

How about you? Do you see yourself as someone of infinite value? God has called you, and *God don't make no junk.* If God called you, He had an incredible reason for doing so. He has a magnificent purpose for your life that He wants you to fulfill. The minute that divine call comes, however, the struggle begins — the struggle to see that call worked out in your life despite the weakness of your humanity and every enemy that might be brought against you.

You may not presently be in a fighting moment. You may simply be in a place where you need to know how to "find the handle" and hang on till the answer comes. This is that place of interim spiritual commitments. It is not an aggressive moment, but one in which your challenge is to simply *stand* and commit yourself to act on the words of Psalm 143:5 and 6. Take them one by one: "I *meditate;* I *remember;* I *muse;* I *ponder;* I *stretch out my hands;* I *pray* for rain like a thirsty desert. These are things I can do!"

Or you may be in a place in your spiritual walk where God wants you to begin waging war through intercession for His purposes to be achieved in your life or in the life of your church. You may be tired of seeing the devil throw you or your church around. It is time for intercession to begin in earnest so you or your church can move into God's fullest purposes!

Perhaps in reading this you have come to question whether or not you are a vassal of Jesus Christ. Perhaps you have no *covenant* relationship with Him. You may know about Him. You may even be a good person with a higher set of moral standards than most other people. Nevertheless, you may never have made a covenant relationship with Jesus Christ. He is not *your* God. You are not *His* vassal. You can't say as this psalmist does: "You are my Lord. I want You to protect me, to stand with me." Instead, you have to admit, "I'm not under that protection."

It isn't so much what you believe, but what you know in your heart. To enter that place of covenant relationship, you must become a vassal of Jesus Christ through *surrender.* Romans 10:9,10 gives us a simple formula for this act of surrender:

...**If you confess with your mouth the Lord Jesus and believe in your heart that God has raised Him from the dead, you will be saved.**

For with the heart one believes unto righteousness, and with the mouth confession is made unto salvation.

I often sing to myself the words of an old black spiritual: "I have decided to follow Jesus. No turning back, no turning back." This is the commitment of surrender every one of us must make in order to enter into covenant relationship with the God who protects, delivers, and helps us finish our course with joy!

Prayer of Commitment

Let us end this important study on the Psalms of penitence with a prayer:

Father, You know the spiritual place I occupy today. I pray that the guidance of Your Word, the comfort of Your Spirit, and the strength and determination that comes from You would separate me from all that has to do with the past. Help me toward the fulfillment of Your purpose in my life. Like the Lord Jesus Christ, I pray that nothing would keep me from finishing the work You have called me to do. Complete that work in me, Lord.

I pray for my enemies, Lord, who may not even know what they are doing when they stand against Your will and purpose in my life. Father, protect me from my enemies until that work is finished. I take comfort in the knowledge that I am Your servant and You are my God. I know that relationship exists. I confirm it and declare that nothing the devil says or my weakness allows will ever separate me from the unchangeable covenant You have made with me. I commit myself to walk in the fullness of Your purpose. In Jesus' Name. Amen.

Appendices
to
Seven Biblical Steps to Personal Renewal

The Power and Practice of Lent

Lent has, for one of its purposes, the preparation for Good Friday and Easter; for Good Friday, when we think of the Body of Jesus taken down from the Cross, and placed in the new tomb, which had been hewn out in the rock (S. Matt. xxvii.60); and for Easter Day when we come to receive that same dear body in the Holy Communion, and to lay it in the tomb of our hearts, hearts so hard and rocky by nature, — may we not use this Collect as a prayer, that our Lenten discipline may so wear away a place in our hard hearts, that when we come at Easter to receive our Lord, those hearts may be "new and contrite," a place hewn out for the Body of our Lord? And then surely we may learn even from the enemies of Jesus, and seal the stone (S. Matt. xxvii. 66) with a good resolution, and set a watch, lest our spiritual foes steal Him away while we sleep, by tempting us in our unwatchful moments to fall again into our old sins.[1]

> — Alfred G. Mortimer
> *Notes on the Seven Penitential Psalms*

Since the time of Origen, Seven Psalms have received the name of Penitential Psalms. They were placed together in the Roman Breviary; and Pope Innocent III ordered their recitation at Lent. Indulgences were promised to those who recited them. One historical allusion may be cited. "In his sick chamber at Hippo, Augustine lay dying. It was a plain and barely furnished room in which he lay. The Penitential Psalms, however, were by his order written out, and placed where he could see them from his bed. These he looked at and read in his days of sickness, weeping often and sore. Thus with his eyes fixed upon the Psalms, Augustine passed to his rest, August 28th, 430."[2]

— Prothero

The Christian Practice of Lent

*A*lthough there is evidence of the Penitential Psalms being used even in the practice of Israel's faith, these Psalms have most recently been a syllabus for the time of "Lent" in the Christian calendar. Although Lent is not observed by many evangelical Christians because they associate it with "high church" liturgical worship, it is being rediscovered by other evangelicals as a means of refocusing their spirituality in an increasingly secular culture.

The History of Lent

One writer said, "Currently Lent is about as high a priority for most people as defrosting their freezer."[3] How tragic! From the time of Christ's apostles, Lent has been a period of preparation and fasting observed before the great Easter festival. However, more people today can identify Mardi Gras, the fling before the fast, than they can the purpose of the fast itself. This is indeed a tragedy!

The word "Lent" comes from the Middle English or Teutonic word *lenten*, which means "spring." The time period is mentioned in Canon 5 of the first ecumenical Council of Nicaea in 325. An even earlier account is found in the Apostolic Tradition (c. 200) of Hippolytus. From these traditions, we know that the season was used both for preparation of candidates for baptism and for restoration of "grievous sinners" who had been excluded from Communion.

By the ninth century when such public penance began to die out, it became customary to remind *all* the faithful of their need for penitence. The practice of placing ashes on each person's forehead on the first day of Lent as a symbol of repentance gave rise to the name Ash Wednesday.

Why 40 Days?
That's a Long Time!

Forty days ultimately comes from the example of Moses, Elijah and certainly Jesus Christ Himself. Our Lord fasted 40 days and 40 nights in the desert, showing plainly enough (if not by express commandment) that the principle of fasting so frequently ordered by God under the Law of the Old Covenant was also to be practiced by the children of the New Covenant.

Because Sunday, the day of celebration and resurrection, was never a fast day, the season of Lent in the Christian church has generally been exactly 40 days over the ages, excluding the six Sundays during Lent. There has been some disagreement between Eastern and Western churches on the dates of the Lent season, but the pattern of its practice is always the same.

In summary, the season of Lent, originating in the fourth-century church, spans 40 weekdays, beginning with Ash Wednesday and climaxing during Holy Week with Maundy Thursday, Good Friday, and its conclusion on the Saturday before Easter.

What Are We To Do?

Jesus spent His 40 days in the wilderness preparing for His ministry by facing the temptations that could potentially cause Him to abandon His calling and ultimate mission. Christians today use the period of Lent for introspection, self-examination and repentance.

Lent is a time period during which special focus should be given to prayer and preparation in order to truly celebrate Easter. The Christian identifies with Christ's temptations in the wilderness as an example of their own "wilderness experiences" in life. *The use of the seven Penitential Psalms during Lent has been a focus of the Christian church since the beginning.*

One recent author has written the following about the season of Lent:

It is too easy and promotes too cheap a grace to focus only on the high points of Palm Sunday and Easter without walking with Jesus through the Darkness of Good Friday, a journey that begins on Ash Wednesday. Lent is a way to place ourselves before God humbled, bringing in our hands no price whereby we can ourselves purchase our salvation. It is a way to confess our total inadequacy before God, to strip ourselves bare of all pretense to righteousness, to come before God in dust and ashes. It is a way to empty ourselves of our false pride, of our rationalizations that prevent us from seeing ourselves as needy creatures, of our "perfectionist" tendencies that blind us to the beam in our own eyes."[4]

Perhaps your question is about *the fast* of the Lent season. What does it include, and how is it walked out? From the time of the earliest church records, personal discretion and individual decision has been honored in the answering of these questions.

The historian Socrates (not to be confused with the fourth-century B.C. Greek philosopher) describes the practice of fasting during Lent in the fifth century:

Some abstain from every sort of creature that has life, while others of all the living creatures eat of fish only. Others eat birds as well as fish, because, according to the Mosaic account of the Creation, they too sprang from the water; others abstain from fruit covered by a hard shell and from eggs. Some eat dry bread only, others not even that; others again when they have fasted to the ninth hour (three o'clock) partake of various kinds of food.[5]

An excellent article in *The Catholic Encyclopedia* by Herbert Thurston deals in a specifically conclusive manner on this subject:

Amid this diversity some inclined to the extreme limits of rigor. Epiphanius, Palladius, and the author of the "Life of St. Melania the Younger" seems to contemplate a state of things in which ordinary Christians were expected to pass twenty-four hours or more without food of any kind, especially during Holy Week, while the more austere actually subsisted during part or the whole of Lent upon one or two meals a week (see Rampolla, "Vita di. S. Melania Giuniore," appendix xxv, p. 478). But the ordinary rule on fasting days was to take but one meal a day and that only in the evening, while meat and, in the early centuries, wine were entirely forbidden.[6]

It is from all these types of backgrounds that the concept of "giving up" something for Lent has come. Indeed, a fast may specifically exclude certain foods, beverages, or certain activities for this period of time.

A writer named Stephanie Salter, whom I have previously quoted, stopped me in my tracks by the following statement: "The point of Lent isn't skipping lunch on Friday. The point of Lent is to contemplate the big picture." She then continued, "What do you suppose Jesus was doing there in the desert for 40 days when he was being tempted by the devil? He was thinking big picture."[7] What a revelation of true repentance!

Historically, Lent was seen as much as a time for almsgiving (charity) as it was for fasting. Lent was meant to secure the calmness and peace of mind that is necessary for true self-examination, repentance, and restored intimacy with God. Therefore, making Lent a time of fasting from amusements, entertainment, or even sports must be considered.

Our focus in Lent is that we are disciples of Jesus Christ and therefore must be reminded of priorities and commitments. One very contemporary minister, as quoted by Stephanie Salter, said that Lent is for "breaking mesmerizing routines."[8] What a concept!

Mesmerizing routines are the activities and behavior patterns that we have become so used to doing that we simply follow them around without thinking throughout our lives. Therefore, Lent might involve a decision about how we use charge cards; how we respond to other drivers on the road; or the presence of gossip in our conversation. Or perhaps we decide to carry two dollars worth of quarters with us during the 40 days of Lent so we can do something nice even for panhandlers. As Stephanie Salter says in her article about Lent: "The point is to break the routine, clear the view, give yourself the chance to think about something besides paying bills, looking sexy, getting ahead or toeing the line."[9]

Lent is really what we want to make of it. However, it is a clear annual opportunity to break the hold of anything in our lives that has become wrongly habitual or controlling.

When the apostle Paul wrote, "All things are lawful for me...," he quickly added, "...but not all things are profitable. *All things are lawful for me, but I will not be mastered by anything*" (1 Corinthians 6:12 *NASB*). Therefore, Lent is an annual time to declare anew, by whatever means chosen, that *only* Jesus Christ is The Lord of our lives.

Preparation and Celebration[1]

VITAL WORSHIP FOR LENT, HOLY WEEK, AND EASTER FROM A 'BLENDED WORSHIP' PERSPECTIVE

By Dan Wagner

Why Lent?

*D*epending on the style and background of a congregation, the idea of observing the Lenten season and Holy Week can bring reactions varying from disdain, criticism, and misunderstanding, to the comfort of familiarity. In congregations which are part of the "free" tradition the idea of observing Lent and Holy Week can be threatening, and subject to mis-characterization and denominational prejudices. And where Lent and Holy Week are familiar observances, there can also be some misunderstandings. Some traditions might need to be examined, refreshed and reconsidered. Congregations of many styles and traditions can learn much by looking at this essential part of the church year. There are many opportunities for creativity which will help make this season a time of spiritual vitality in worship.

If the idea of observing Lent, or even "Holy Week," are threatening to the congregation or its leadership, it is wise to move carefully and circumspectly in introducing these ideas. A basic grasp of the importance and purpose of the season is required. Perhaps even use of the term "Lent" will be too threatening for some congregations, but that need not hinder the congregation from benefiting spiritually from the richness of the concept. To make the observance meaningful, the worship planner must look beyond the superficial clichés of somberness, and of "giving something up for Lent." While Lent may be a wonderful opportunity to emphasize occasions of quietness, reflection and self-examination in worship, there need not be an abandonment of the overall worship mood of a congregation. In fact, if observing the Church Year is unfamiliar to a congregation, a drastic stylistic change during Lent would probably be unwise. And, although the discipline of "giving something up" might be a concept that would enhance the spiritual disciplines of the evangelical believer (it might be better known as a "fast" — a thoroughly biblical discipline), the "giving up" idea might be better left unmentioned for the congregation still in the process of discovering the value of the season.

Worship and Discipleship Through Lent

There is much potential for developing an overall worship emphasis for the season of Lent. It can be a time when the personal spiritual disciplines of the follower of Jesus Christ are emphasized. It can be a time when a fuller examination of the riches of the grace of Christ are emphasized. It might be a time of more focused reflection upon the personal relationships of the believer. Honesty with God, one's neighbor and with one's family and friends could be the theme. Materials for discipleship from organizations such as Navigators or Chapel of the Air's "50 Day Spiritual Adventure" could be used. The ideal approach, of course, is a synergistic approach to worship and sermon planning. A sermon series related to any of the above worship themes, or a series related to the key spiritual issues brought forward by the appointed texts, can be very effective.

To investigate the meaning of the Lenten season, an excellent place to begin is in the Revised Common Lectionary. While this suggestion might be received with some hesitancy, it is important to realize that, in the "free" worship tradition, liturgical tradition may be incorporated, modified, or simply used to inform and enrich worship. Surely, the variety of readings from the Scriptures can only serve to bring life to worship. Many of the finest themes of scripture abound in the assigned readings. Each week features a compelling story of people of God from the Old Testament which foreshadows the New Covenant, the beauty of some of the most familiar penitential psalms is expressed, great New Testament teachings on the essence of salvation and righteousness are presented and Christ's own words about his coming atonement are voiced. The season is rich in theology and filled with opportunities for personal application.

An excellent annual resource for study of the "assigned" readings is a book by Bone and Scifres, titled *Music and Worship Planner* (Abingdon Press, Nashville, TN). This book contains the appointed scriptures of the day, printed out, and on the opposing page, suggests hymns, choral music and other musical ideas that enhance the readings. Even in a church which incorporates very "contemporary" worship music, these seeds of ideas for worship can be universal and relevant.

Of course, the season of Lent is brought to exciting culmination in the celebration of Holy Week. The worship sequence of Palm Sunday, Maundy (Holy) Thursday, Good Friday and Easter (Resurrection) Sunday, is laden with potential for the finest feast of worship of the year. These observances explore the depths of the greatest points of Christian theology, the deepest human emotion and the impact of salvation itself. At least *some* elements of this celebration seem almost essential in establishing the true, historically Christian nature of the congregation.

While there will always be debate over the use of the church year in worship and the extent to which these seasons are observed, much can be gained by a look at the observances, and a discussion of some practical worship planning ideas which relate to the appointed scriptures and spiritual principles suggested for a given event. For the purposes of this article, resources for the "blended" or "contemporary" worship style will be given greater emphasis. The reason for this emphasis might be obvious — churches which are liturgical in focus are very likely to have access to plenty of traditional worship resources for choir and congregation which are designed to enhance the Lenten and Holy Week observances. Even in those congregations however, an overview of some materials from nontraditional sources might provide some fresh surprises to what might otherwise be a comfortable liturgical tradition. The worship leader who is unaccustomed to observing Lent in worship might be pleasantly surprised at how universally applicable and challenging the appointed themes and texts can be.

Worship Ideas for Lent

The following ideas are based on this year's assigned scripture readings from the Revised Common Lectionary, and additional general concepts related to the special observances:

Ash Wednesday

Certainly, Ash Wednesday will never be an option for some churches. But a study of this liturgical event will reveal a depth and richness which can be exciting fuel for worship planning. The tradition of the imposition of ashes is a physical symbol of our mortality, and, by implication, the burning up of all that is of human effort — and the application of the sacrifice of Christ as a covering for sin. It is a service that looks not only inwardly and introspectively, but "upward," to the miracles of grace and mercy. Temporary introspection in the worship event must always lead the believer to a refreshing glimpse of grace and forgiveness. This is one of the most important concepts of Lent. For congregations which would be hesitant to adopt this liturgical observance (and there are many), the principles of this service can still teach us ways to prepare for Holy Week and strengthen our devotion.

The appointed scripture readings for Ash Wednesday are:

Joel 2:1-2,12-17 — *"Blow the trumpet in Zion... return to me with all your heart..."* — A solemn call to spiritual readiness.

Psalm 51 — A beloved passage of penitential scripture.

2 Corinthians 5:20b-6:10 — Reconciliation is offered with Christ. Christ's righteousness on our behalf, our willingness to abandon ourselves.

Matthew 6:1-6,16-21 — A reminder that spiritual rewards come from what is done privately, not publicly.

The Sundays and Weeks of Lent

There is not complete agreement among liturgical traditions as to the implications of the Lenten Season in weekly worship. Two good concepts seem to be at odds. Often in Christian worship, every Sunday is thought to be a "little Easter" — a celebration of the Risen Christ. But the discipline of Lent, including liturgical concepts such as "no Alleluias," would seem to work against the "little Easter." Of course, the answer can be to look at the season both ways. True repentance in the Christian life is an encounter with ultimate Truth and complete Love. Likewise, the penitential aspects of worship emphasize the demands of discipleship, but should always be a journey toward a victory of which we are certain. There is an understanding that the resurrection has indeed already occurred, and joy is always offered to the believer as a fruit of the Spirit.

Midweek Lenten Services

In churches which include midweek Lenten services in their calendars, drama and music can help make these services interesting. Both contemporary and biblical drama can be used. For music ministries which tend to be "stretched thin," monologues for each Lenten service can be wonderful. Little time is demanded of the leadership, but the results are extremely rewarding for the congregation. One possible theme is a monologue each week from a character involved in the Holy Week events. Such monologues are readily available from drama publishing houses. Also, Lenten devotional guides may be created using devotional thoughts compiled by the church pastor(s), elders or deacons, teachers or other leaders. Other ideas for these services might be to include youth or other special soloists, or, if the church facility allows, to invite an area choir, boy's choir, community chorus, handbell choir — any high-quality ensemble to perform at the Lenten service. Many of these groups are looking for community outreach opportunities. (Of course it is important to have input as to the repertoire being used, ensuring its appropriateness for the service.)

Scriptures and Themes
for the Five Sundays of Lent

Lent 1 — A unified worship theme which points the way from judgment to salvation and righteousness —

Genesis 9:8-17 — God's judgment and covenant established.

Psalm 25:1-10 — The soul lifted to God, God responds with faithfulness.

1 Peter 3:18-22 — A "creed" statement on salvation and baptism.

Mark 1:9-15 — Jesus' baptism, the kingdom of God is near, repent and believe.

Lent 2 — God's promises to Abraham and to us —

Genesis 17:1-7, 15-16 — God promises to bless Abraham and his descendants.

Psalm 22:23-31 — "Offspring of Jacob, glorify Him"...future generations will glorify the Lord.

Romans 4:13-25 — Abraham's righteousness, and ours, are by faith.

Mark 8:31-38 — Christ begins to tell of his upcoming suffering — we are to take up our cross.

Lent 3 — The readings of this day sharply juxtapose the law of the Lord, and the coming fulfillment of the law in Christ —

Exodus 20:1-17 — The ten commandments.

Psalm 19 — Heavens declare God's glory, God's law is perfect, aspiration for, and confession to God.

1 Corinthians — The message of the cross is foolishness to those who perish.

John 2:13-22 — Christ clears the temple, and tells of his coming resurrection.

Lent 4 — A powerful exposition of salvation is the theme of this Sunday.

Numbers 21:4-9 — God's people are judged for speaking against the Lord, and saved by looking to God's redemption.

Psalm 107:1-3, 17-22 — God's forgiveness and healing leads to joy.

Ephesians 2:1-10 — Clear presentation of salvation by grace.

John 3:14-21 — Christ, our salvation (as typified in the Numbers passage).

Lent 5 — The covenant is God's law on our hearts, and is fulfilled and personified in Christ.

Jeremiah 31:31-34 — The new covenant: God's law written on our hearts.

Psalm 51:1-12 — A magnificent penitential Psalm.

Hebrews 5:5-10 — Christ's humanity in suffering, and his High Priesthood, fulfilling the law (cf. Jeremiah).

John 12:20-33 — Christ reveals more about his coming sacrifice and glorification.

Worship Ideas for Holy Week

There are many ways in which this most significant Christian sequence is observed. Beginning with Palm Sunday, traditions abound. Usually the theme is centered around the Triumphal Entry, with palms present in various forms, and plenty of exciting "Hosanna's." Easter Sunday might be celebrated with the congregation's favorite hymn or two with lots of fanfare and Alleluias. In some churches the entire content of the salvation event is compacted into the Easter Sunday observance. Sermons on the cross sometimes are the fare for Easter Sunday. But a review of the historic pattern of Holy Week celebration will reveal possibilities for a much more thorough understanding of the week's events. When understanding is deepened, devotion and celebration are enhanced in meaning and intensity. Again, an overview of the Lectionary readings is very revealing. Even if these are not used in their entirety, they provide an outstanding underpinning for worship and music planning. When spiritual principles are involved, it is almost always a profound experience as events and concepts are viewed with deeper care, and in the light of scripture.

Scriptures and Themes for Holy Week
Palm Sunday
(also known as 'Passion Sunday')

Palm Sunday is an excellent opportunity to recreate the excitement of Christ's Triumphal Entry, and the dramatic shift in public sentiment that would quickly lead to His crucifixion. Services might begin with great shouts of celebration, but even a small portion of the service looking ahead to Good Friday can be highly effective. In fact, the very logical emotional "shape" of this day, from triumph to passion, is a stirring, compact statement of truth in time and space. How well prepared the congregation would be to receive the Word, and to continue in worship through the rest of the Holy Week!

Mark 11:1-11 — St. Mark's gospel narrative of the Triumphal Entry.

Psalm 118:1-2, 19-29 — A psalm of jubilant praise illuminating the Hebrew response of worship, foreshadowing the Palm Sunday events.

(Alternate Passion) Psalm 31:9-16 — Prophetic of Christ's suffering.

Isaiah 50:4-9a — Prophecy of the crucifixion.

Philippians 2:5-11 — "Let this mind be in you"...one of the great theological passages in the New Testament on the doctrine of Christ.

(alternate Gospel reading) Mark 14:1-15:47 — the complete Passion according to St. Mark.

Maundy (Holy) Thursday and Good Friday

These two days of observance during Holy Week have two distinct themes, which lend themselves to varied expressions in worship. Practical considerations or simple custom may lead many congregations to forego observing one or the other. However, once the congregation understands what the entire Holy Week worship experience can be like, there is often plenty of motivation to celebrate each of the events. If practical considerations are a hindrance, i.e., human resources and time, one might consider employing significant use of drama, small vocal groups, soloists, instrumentalists, lay speakers or leaders. There are many alternatives to requiring the church choir to lead in both weeknight observances.

The Last Supper is the main event of Maundy Thursday. For this reason, communion can be much more meaningful here than at the Good Friday service. The Last Supper is a highly visual event, which lends itself easily to drama in the form of tableaus or a "Living Last Supper" format. Drama can include speaking, but speaking is not required. Creative portrayal of communion itself, unique and artistic presentations around the table, and variations from the normal communion routine can be highly effective on Maundy Thursday. This is a good day for freshly baked matzo, and other tangible or visual worship aids. The gathering of the disciples for Passover can bring a unique Jewish flavor to this service. Music can have a different style on Thursday to distinguish it clearly from Friday. Some congregations might wish to make Maundy Thursday more "contemporary," musically speaking, while Good Friday might have a more reflective mood. Rereading of the Last Supper narrative will spark lots of creative ideas. Servanthood and love for one another are very important themes of the Maundy Thursday observance. The eschatological theme "Maranatha, Lord Jesus, quickly come" may also be highlighted. The congregation will eventually sense that the story is incomplete without both worship times.

Scripture for Maundy Thursday

Exodus 12:1-4, 11-14 — Passover.

Psalm 116:1-4, 12-19 — Prophetic of Christ's death, and thanksgiving in the face of suffering.

1 Corinthians 11:23-26 — The "words of institution" of the communion celebration.

John 13:1-17, 31b-35 — St. John's Gospel narrative of the Last Supper. Very rich in themes for worship!

Good Friday

Good Friday's focus is the Passion of Christ. Ways to lead this worship experience are plentiful. The choral repertoire for the Passion story is almost endless in virtually every worship and music style. One need not shy away from the reflective weightiness of Good Friday. Hope is woven throughout the service, but it is highly appropriate to linger at the cross for this relatively short period of time. Communication to the congregation of the nature of this service is important. Those who may not be ready for this kind of reflection need to know what to expect. In dealing with the theme of the Passion, however, sensitivity to pacing and musical selection will help in keeping the focus and pacing just right. If the congregation loves 19th century gospel hymns, or praise choruses, it is important to include some of what they love in the service. (There is much in these genres on the passion theme.) Stylistic inclusiveness, with sensitivity to the mood of the service, will open hearts and encourage receptive minds for other kinds of expressions.

Nonmusical factors are also important. The historic tenebrae format can be amazingly thought-provoking and captivating. (Again, refer to available liturgical and drama resources available.) The use of gradually extinguished candlelight, with the last light eventually taken out of the room for a moment can have an inestimable impact. Themes of the "Seven Last Words," or the "Stations of the Cross" will invite creative worship ideas. Again, staff members, or lay leaders could prepare very brief reflections at prescribed juncture points. Or, the scriptural narration, well read, will be more than effective. Interspersing well prepared anthems, solos, ensemble selections and hymns will enhance the drama. Revisiting the liturgical passions of the great composers will also provide ideas for worship. The Bach passions, for instance, with their interwoven narrative commentary, and highly personal responses are still profound sources of inspiration and understanding for our worship on Good Friday. But musical genre matters little. Capturing the essence of the day is much more important. To do this, there is no good substitute for the profound simplicity of the appointed scriptures of the day.

Isaiah 52:13-53:12 — Prophetic and poetic, this passage will inspire many musical choices.

Psalm 22 — Prophesies the crucifixion, ends with the promise of salvation.

Hebrews 10:16-25 — The new covenant and words of challenge and encouragement.

John 18:1-19:42 — The Passion according to St. John.

Easter Sunday

Perhaps because it is more broadly accepted in worship tradition, less might need to be said about Easter Sunday. If a congregation grows in their worship and understanding of Lent and the rest of Holy Week, it is important to remember that Easter is a *resurrection celebration*. Quite often the worship materials chosen will reflect either the cross, or the glorified Christ. These themes are wonderful before and after, but the challenge is to find the plentiful choices which focus specifically on the fact that Christ conquered death. Congregations respond well to the excitement of Resurrection Sunday, and enjoy lots of color, life and enthusiasm. Children's choirs are often an excellent addition to the service. Easter celebration certainly calls for "pulling out all the stops," but the pastoral musician might also place a slight emphasis on some of the tender aspects of the resurrection account — Christ's gentle encounter with Mary, for instance, and the emphasis on the new life which believers encounter.

Easter Sunday Scriptures

Acts 10:34-43 — The apostle Peter tells the gospel.

Psalm 118:1-2, 14-24 — A psalm celebrating new life...this is the day the Lord has made!

1 Corinthians 15:1-11 — Statement of the resurrection gospel and salvation by grace.

John 20:1-18 — The resurrection account from St. John.

Liturgically-oriented readers will notice the absence of discussion of the Easter Vigil Service. This meaningful part of Holy Week is observed in many churches, and if it is unfamiliar to the reader, a good reference would be Robert Webber's *The Complete Library of Christian Worship*, Vol. 5, *The Services of the Christian Year* (Star Song/Abbott-Martyn Press). In fact, this volume will offer many ideas for worship through Lent, Holy Week and the entire Church year.

An additional catalyst for worship planning is the idea that Easter is a six-week season, not just one Sunday. While some congregations would not respond well to the most familiar resurrection hymns on the following Sundays, this extended "Eastertide" is excellent for use of the many hymns that deal with the Resurrected and living Christ. (Consider "I Know That My Redeemer Lives," "Jesus Lives and So Shall I," "I Serve A Risen Savior," "Crown Him With Many Crowns," "Thine Be the Glory," etc.) Additionally, choral selections, solos and ensembles might make good use of a true follow-up in worship to the celebration of the Risen Lord.

The challenge, joy and privilege of those involved in music and worship leadership is to approach the empty-page of worship planning week after week, and to take up the sacred responsibility of helping our congregations address God, and to experience God as He really is. While we will never fully accomplish this in our earthly limitations, we can gain much from studying and enjoying the worship of other traditions and other times in history. Sometimes, the very spark of life that is longed for in our worship is found in a denomination or tradition that in the past has been viewed with disdain. To consider the wisdom of others that have traditionally been considered "them" and "not us" can reveal some priceless gems. Although the terminology of the church year and the structure that goes with it may be foreign to many fine churches, there is much to be discovered there. One of the positive aspects of our eclectic culture allows for adaptation, modification and fresh approaches to what is excellent from the past. It is, indeed, essential to pursue this rich heritage.

Musical Selections for Lent and Holy Week
A Few Lenten Choral Suggestions

Lord, I want To Be A Christian (trad./arr. Laster) Augsburg #11-1739

Followers of the Lamb (arr. Dietterich) Agape #AG-7223

Deep Within (GIA)

Jesus, Lamb of God (Michael Joncas)

We Remember

Broken for Me

Come to the Table: Medley (various, arr. O. D. Hall) Integrity #4114OC

There Is A Redeemer

Praise Choruses for Palm Sunday or Resurrection Celebration

For This Purpose (Kendrick)

Lift High the Lord

Victory Chant

All Heaven Declares

Shout to the Lord

Almighty

He Is Lovely

Celebrate Jesus Celebrate

I Know That My Redeemer Lives
(possibly sung in folk style)

Good Friday Choral or Ensemble Repertoire (Blended Style)

Written In Red (Jensen/Kirkland)
Word #301-0662-165

Hallelujah, Praise the Lamb (McSpadden/
Thomas/arr. Christopher) Word #301-0522-169

I Surrender All (Venter/arr. Mark Hayes)
Flammer #A-6791

When I Survey the Wondrous Cross
(arr. Gilbert Martin) Presser #312-40785

To the Cross (Adams/Mason/arr. Kirkland)
Word #301-0756-16X — w/med. solo

The Holy Heart (Praise Band 4) SAT ensemble or
Octavo arr.

Lamb of God (Paris) — various version

Post-Easter (Eastertide) Music Suggestions (Blended style)

The Lamb Has Overcome (Carol Cymbala) Word
#301-0786-166

Honored, Glorified, Exalted (Vader/Rouse/arr.
Kirkland) Praise Gathering #AO8116

The Majesty and Glory of Your Name
(Tom Fettke) Word #301-0122-160

Holy Is He (Clydesdale) Word #301-0506-162

Thou Art Worthy (Cindy Berry)
Word #301-0494-165

Alleluia (Ralph Manuel) Hinshaw #HMC-927

Alleluia (Randall Thompson E. C. Schirmer #1228

Sample Services for Lent, Holy Week, and Eastertide

I have included several service designs from Crystal Evangelical Free Church, New Hope, Minnesota. These specific services are not presented here for anyone to use "as is," but to assist others in their planning and thinking.

First, a few notes about the "Living Last Supper" service. This service began as an outgrowth of the Maranatha compilation called "The Feast" (now out of print, but some music dealers may have stock copies). Drama was added and integrated into the narration. The biblical account was researched, and the gospel accounts were cross-referenced. The dramatic script, "I Am The Vine" (Lillenas #MP672) was later incorporated into one year's presentation. Scenic flats were constructed and painted as a rustic stone wall. (Draped fabric might work as well.) The table is set with "biblical" props, food items, rich fabrics, etc. Action takes place in the aisles, and in front of, or behind the table. The worship ensemble and instrumentalists (we use a 5-piece contemporary group) are off stage for this event. The focus is on the table throughout the service. Theatrical lighting is a very helpful addition, using rich colors, and gradually changing the mood toward "evening."

Repent, or Else...[1]

By Campbell McAlpine

"God Now Commands
All Men Everywhere To Repent."[2]

*a*t the beginning of the twentieth century, William Booth, the founder of the Salvation Army, expressed his fears for the future. He foresaw the dangers of "a religion without the Holy Spirit; Christianity without Christ; salvation without regeneration; heaven without hell and forgiveness without repentance." His fears were well-founded.

The preaching of John the Baptist and the preaching of Jesus commenced with the call to 'repent.'

John Milton said, "Repentance is the golden key that opens the palace of eternity. The gate of God's kingdom is closed to those who refuse to repent."

True repentance is not merely an acknowledgement of sin, but a forsaking of sin, as Isaiah proclaimed, *"Let the wicked forsake his way, and the unrighteous man his thoughts, let him return to the Lord."*[3]

Repentance is a clean break from selfish, sinful living. John Bunyan asked the question, "Wilt thou leave thy sins and go to Heaven, or wilt thou have thy sins and go to hell?"[4]

Why do Christians Need to Repent?

"Repent, or else…" These words were not spoken by some wild-eyed, publicity-seeking, arm-waving eccentric…but by Jesus Christ, the Son of the Living God.

Jesus had died, risen from the dead and ascended to the right hand of the Majesty on high. He had loved the Church and given Himself for her. The Church had experienced the blessing of the Day of Pentecost and had gone everywhere preaching the dynamic Gospel, the power of God unto salvation. There had been 'signs following' such proclamation, with accompanying persecution, imprisonment and martyrdom. However, the Mighty God was with them. Nations were reached, Churches were established as His servants declared the Good News that through Christ, man could have relationship with God, forgiveness of sins, eternal life and the enabling of the Holy Spirit to do and enjoy the will of God.

In time, the zeal of some of the Churches had abated. There was the intrusion of wrong teaching, counterfeit ministries, wrong priorities, resulting in a pattern without power, formality without fervour, activity without achievement. To such Churches, Jesus the Head of the Church pleads, "Repent, or else..."

Today we hear the repetition of certain words, good words: Renewal...Restoration...Revival... However, all these can never be truly experienced without another word: Repentance.

Repentance is a condition of God's forgiveness and restoration to favour. Isaiah describes it as *"washing ourselves, making ourselves clean, putting away the evil of our doings, ceasing to do evil, learning to be good."*[5]

Christians need to repent! A good question to ask ourselves is: "When did I last confess a sin and repent of it? When did I last apologize? When did I last make restitution? Have I really lived sinless all that time?"

Christians Need to Repent Because Christians Sin.

Christians need not sin, but let's face it, sometimes we do.

Thomas Carlyle said, "The greatest of all faults is to be conscious of none."

John wrote, *If anyone sins, we have an advocate with the Father, Jesus Christ the righteous.*[6] Sin is meant to be the exception and not the rule.

Paul clearly states, *"Sin shall not have dominion over you.*[7] He asks the question, *"How shall we who are dead to sin live any longer therein?"*[8] No one can truthfully say "I cannot sin," but a Christian can say: "I need not sin." Again, Paul reminds us that we have been *"crucified with Christ."*[9] That old Adamic nature need not have the victory over me.

I saw a lot of dead men in war. I never heard a dead man criticize or judge another. I never heard a dead man lie. I never saw a dead man commit adultery or fornication. They couldn't...they were dead!

We are exhorted to *"Reckon yourselves dead unto sin, and alive unto God."*[10] We never sin without first being tempted to sin and with every temptation there is always a way of escape. We have the ability by God's help to say "No"!

Christians Need to Repent to be Forgiven.

One of the meanings of repentance is to "turn from." There must be a willingness, not only to acknowledge our sins and confess them, but also to turn from them. To confess a sin with the intention of doing the same thing again, is meaningless. True repentance has the determination to put away the sin.

Paul exhorted the Ephesians to *"put away lying, don't give place to the devil; steal no more; stop corrupt communications coming from your mouths; put away bitterness, evil speaking, malice."*[11]

Repentance is turning to God with a willingness to turn from sin. It produces a cry like David's, *"Have mercy on me, O God."*[12] It is completely honest and takes personal responsibility. It doesn't blame circumstances or people. Repentance is a prerequisite to forgiveness. *"Repent...that your sins may be blotted out."*[13]

Christians Need to Repent To Enjoy Fellowship with God.

Sin separates us from God. It spoils our fellowship with Him, even though we have a relationship with Him. The truly repentant realizes that sin is against God. David cried, *"I acknowledge my transgressions and my sin is ever before me. Against You, and You only have I sinned, and done this evil in Your sight."*[14] The prodigal son declared, *"I have sinned against heaven."*[15]

It is not mere regret, which is what we feel when we realize what we have done to ourselves. It is not remorse, which is what we feel we have done to others. Repentance is what we feel when we realize what we have done to God. Sin grieves Him. Repentance is necessary for restoration of fellowship with Him. It is His goodness that leads us to repentance.

Conviction of sin is an evidence of God's love for us. *"As many as I love I rebuke and chasten; be zealous and repent."*[16] True repentance will be evidenced by its fruit. We will not only get right with God, but also with others. We will say sorry and ask for forgiveness from those we have hurt. We will return things to their rightful owners. We will pay our debts.

The word "repent" is often followed by the word "and," i.e., *"Repent **and** believe the Gospel."*[17] *"Repent **and** be baptized."*[18] *"Repent **and** turn to God."*[19] *"Repent **and** do the first works."*[20]

What joy there is in fellowship and intimacy with our God and Father and His gloriously wonderful Son, Jesus.

Christians Need to Repent Because of the Consequences of Not Repenting.

Undealt-with sin usually leads to more sinning. Refusal to repent hardens the heart and sears the conscience and grieves the Holy Spirit. A failure to respond to His convictions is dangerous. *"He who is often reproved and hardens his neck, will suddenly be destroyed and that without remedy."*[21] When the Lord Jesus sent His messages to the Churches in Asia pleading with them to repent, He used the words 'or else.'

To Ephesus who had lost their first love — that is the love that puts Him first, He said, *"Repent, or else I will remove your candlestick."*[22]

To Pergamos, *"Repent, **or else** I will fight against you."*[23]

To Thyatira, *"Repent, **or else** I will send tribulation."*[24]

To Sardis, *"Repent, **or else** I will come as a thief in the night."*[25]

To Laodicea, *"Be zealous and repent, **or else** I will spue you out of My mouth."*[26]

These were not mere threats, but warnings...and God always keeps His word.

Christians Need to Repent So That Nations Might be Blessed.

The oft quoted 2 Chronicles 7:14 reminds us that repentance is a prelude to revival: *"If My people, who are called by My name will humble themselves, and pray, and seek My face, and turn from their wicked ways; then I will hear from heaven, and will forgive their sin, and heal the land."*

A desire for revival is a worthy desire, but desire without repentance is unrealistic. Prayer for revival is right, but prayer from unrepentant hearts does not reach Heaven's Throne.

Listening to sermons on revival, reading articles and books on revival, helpful though they may be, are ineffective without repentance.

Some of us can remember the same interest in revival 40 years ago. There were nights of prayer for revival and sometimes weeks of prayer for revival. We heard thrilling stories of what God had done in Indonesia, in the Congo and on the Isle of Lewis, etc. Yet, revival has not come to our nation.

Instead of being of 'one heart' we have seen divisions, new groupings, new organizations, new conferences, but not Holy Ghost revival!

Instead of being known as the disciples of Jesus Christ by our evident love for one another, our schisms and disagreements denominationally and doctrinally have left many non-Christians unconvinced about our genuineness and beliefs.

Do we have ears to hear? "If my people will...I will."

If Christians Need to Repent...
Do I...Do we?

The old 'spiritual' song said, "It's not my brother or my sister, but me O Lord, standin' in the need of prayer." Repentance starts with me...with you.

"If Any Man Will...I Will."

These words were spoken by Jesus to the Church in Laodicea, after calling on them to repent with the promise of intimate fellowship with Him: *"I will come in to him and dine with him, and he with me."*[27] What a wonderful promise!

How can I repent?

Firstly, deal with every known sin. **Acknowledge** them. **Confess** them. **Repent** of them. **Obey** whatever needs to be done in restitution, (apologies, forgiveness).

Then, borrow David's prayer, *"Search me, O God, and know my heart; try me and know my anxieties; and see if there is any wicked way in me, and lead me in the way everlasting."*[28] Now, be still and let Him answer your prayer, that He might reveal anything of which you have not been conscious.

When we have truly repented, we are assured by His words of comfort and forgiveness: *"Neither do I condemn you, go and sin no more."*[29] There will be joy, too. The joy of fellowship with the Lord; the joy of sins forgiven; the joy of restored fellowship with others and the joy of knowing there is joy in heaven over one sinner who repents.

"If My People Will...I Will."

Many Churches need to repent and get right with God. Repent of pride; of undealt-with sin; of prayerlessness; of sins against leadership and leadership's sins against the people. Repent of disunity; an independent spirit; worldliness and compromise; a lack of loving and scriptural discipline. How much has been "swept under the carpet" only resulting in recurrent problems? "If my people will...I will."

"If That Nation Will...I Will."

God said to the prophet Jeremiah, after giving him an object lesson by watching a Potter at work restoring a marred vessel, "If that nation against whom I have spoken turns from its evil, I will relent of the disaster that I thought to bring upon it."[30] Solemn, yet encouraging words.

As a nation, we have turned from God; despised His commandments; blasphemed His Holy Name; forgotten His past mercies and preservation; failed to acknowledge our need and dependence on Him. We have built our Babel towers and declared by our actions, *"Away with Him, away with Him, we will not have this Man to reign over us."*[31] We are ripe for judgement. The day is fast approaching when men will call on the hills and mountains to *"hide them from the face of Him who sits on the Throne."*[32]

Is it Too Late? Is There Hope?

"If any man will...I WILL."

"If My people will...I WILL."

"If that nation will...I WILL."

Will I? Will you? Will we...repent? Only history will reveal the answer!

Jesus said..."Repent, or else."

Endnotes

Front Matter

[1] Saint Augustine, as quoted by Alfred G. Mortimer in *Notes on the Seven Penitential Psalms* (London and New York: Longmans, Green, and Co., 1895), p. 5.

[2] N. H. Snaith, as quoted by Leslie C. Allen, *Word Biblical Commentary: Psalms 101-150*, Vol. 21 (Waco, Texas: Word Books, 1983), p. 283.

[3] Jack Higgins, *Day of Judgment* (New York: Bantam Book, published by arrangement with Holt, Rinehart, and Winston, 1979), p. 273.

[4] Ibid.

Psalm 6: First of the Penitential Psalms

[1] Mortimer, op. cit., pp. 12,13.

[2] F. B. Meyer, *Bible Commentary* (Wheaton, Illinois: Tyndale House Publishers, 1983), p. 232.

[3] Mortimer, op. cit., p. 14.

Psalm 32: Second of the Penitential Psalms

[1] John Adams, *The Lenten Psalms* (New York: Charles Scribner's Sons, 1912), p. 32.

Psalm 38: Third of the Penitential Psalms

[1] Harry Rimmer, *The Crucible of Calvary*, as quoted by Erling C. Olsen in *Meditations on the Psalms*, Vol. 1 (New York: Noizeaux Brothers, 1941), p. 293.

[2] Alexander MacLaren, *The Complete Biblical Library, Psalms* (Springfield, Missouri: World Library Press, Inc., 1996), p. 176.

[3] Donald M. Williams, *The Communicator's Commentary, Psalms 1-72* (Waco, Texas: Word Books, 1986), p. 290.

[4] Erling C. Olsen, *Meditations in the Psalms*, Vol. 1 (New York: Noizeaux Brothers, 1941), p. 291.

[5] A "Punjabi" is a native of the Punjab region of Northwest India and West Pakistan.

[6] Eugene H. Peterson, *Message Bible* (Colorado Springs: NavPress, 1993), p. 702.

[7] Williams, op. cit., pp. 285,286.

[8] Williams, op. cit., p. 290.

[9] "Rock of Ages." Words by August M. Todlady, 1776. Music by Thomas Hastings, 1830.

Psalm 51: Fourth of the Penitential Psalms

[1] Williams, op. cit., pp. 361,362.

[2] Martin Luther, as quoted by C. H. Spurgeon, *The Treasury of David*, Vol. 1 (Byron Center, Michigan: Associated Publishers, 1970), p. 457.

[2] Williams, op. cit. p. 362.

[3] Franz Joseph Haydn, as quoted by Erling C. Olsen, op. cit., p. 415.

[4] Williams, op. cit., p. 369.

[5] St. Augustine, as quoted by Alfred G. Mortimer, op. cit., p. 62.

Psalm 102: Fifth of the Penitential Psalms

[1] Mortimer, op. cit., p. 135.

[2] Allen, op. cit., p. 11.

[3] Ibid, p. 14.

[4] Lloyd John Ogilvie, *The Bush Is Still Burning* (Waco, Texas: Word Books, 1981), p. 17.

Psalm 130: Sixth of the Penitential Psalms

[1] Arno C. Gaebelein, *The Book of Psalms* (Wheaton, Illinois: Van Kampen Press, 1939), p. 461.

[2] Martin Luther, as quoted by Gaebelein, op. cit., p. 461.

[3] C. Thomas Hilton, *The Clergy Journal* (Austin: March 1988), p. 12.

[4] Dr. Joyce Brothers' column, *Fort Lauderdale Sun Sentinel* (October 1986).

[5] *Good News Bible or The Bible in Today's English Version* (Nashville, New York: Thomas Nelson Publishers, 1976), p. 684.

[6] *The Living Bible*, as included in *The New Layman's Bible* (Grand Rapids: Zondervan, 1981), p. 1589.

Psalm 143: Seventh of the Penitential Psalms

[1] Mortimer, op. cit., pp. 181,182.

[2] N. H. Snaith, as quoted by Leslie C. Allen, op. cit., p. 283.

[3] *Ebenezar* is a location in the Old Testament that literally means "hitherto has the Lord helped me."

[4] Peterson, op. cit., p. 857.

[5] *Revised Standard Version*, Old Testament Section (Division of Christian Education of the National Council of Churches of Christ in the United States of America, 1952).

Appendix 1

[1] Mortimer, op. cit., p. 89.

[2] Prothero, as quoted by John Adams, op. cit., p. viii.

[3] Stephanie Salter, "Have a Nice Lent," *The San Francisco Examiner* (February 23, 1988), p. A-11.

[4] Dennis Bratcher, "The Season of Lent," *The Voice* (Christian Resource Institute, March 2000), http://www.cresourcei.org/cylent.html#Journey, p. 5.

[5] Socrates, as quoted by Herbert Thurston, "Lent," *The Catholic Encyclopedia*, Vol. IX (Robert Appleton Co., 1910; Online Edition, Kevin Knight, 2000), http://www.newadvent.org/cathen/09152a.htm, p. 3.

[6] Ibid.

[7] Salter, op. cit., p. A-11.

[8] Ibid.

[9] Ibid.

Appendix 2

[1] Dan Wagner, "Preparation and Celebration," *Creator Magazine* (San Carlos, California: *Creator Magazine*, 1998), http://www.creatormagazine.com. Reprinted by permission.

Appendix 3

[1] Campbell McAlpine, "Repent, or Else…" This article was written for the Day of National Prayer in Great Britain in 1998. Every member of Parliament, government official, and bishop — even the Queen herself — received a copy. Reprinted by permission.

[2] Acts 17:30

[3] Isaiah 55:7

[4] John Bunyan, as quoted by William Barclay, *Daily Study Bible, The Gospel of Matthew*, Vol. 1 (Philadelphia: The Westminster Press, 1958), p. 43.

[5] Isaiah 1:16

[6] 1 John 2:1

[7] Romans 6:14

[8] Romans 6:2

[9] Galatians 2:20

[10] Romans 6:11

[11] Ephesians 4:28,29

[12] Psalm 51:1

[13] Acts 3:19

[14] Psalm 51:3,4

[15] Luke 15:18

[16] Revelation 3:19

[17] Mark 1:15

[18] Acts 2:38

[19] Ezekiel 4:16

[20] Revelation 2:5

[21] Proverbs 29:1

[22] Revelation 2:5

[23] Revelation 2:16

[24] Revelation 2:22

[25] Revelation 3:3

[26] Revelation 3:19

[27] Revelation 3:20

[28] Psalm 139:23,24

[29] John 8:11

[30] Jeremiah 18:8

[31] John 19:15

[32] Revelation 6:16

Other Book by Rick C. Howard

Songs From Life (hardback)
Strategy for Triumph: A Christian Perspective on Problems
The Finding Times of God
The Judgement Seat of Christ
The Judgement Seat of Christ (Spanish)
The Lost Formula of the Early Church (hardback)

Naioth Sound and Publishing
2995 Woodside Road, Suite 400
Woodside, California 94062
Toll free: 1-800-726-3127
Fax: 1-650-368-0790

Discounts for volume amounts:
40% Discount for bookstores
50% Discount for churches
60% Discount for distributors